BUSINESS MANAGEMENT of GENERAL CONSUMER MAGAZINES

BUSINESS MANAGEMENT of GENERAL CONSUMER MAGAZINES

William Parkman Rankin

PRAEGER

PRAEGER SPECIAL STUDIES • PRAEGER SCIENTIFIC

Library of Congress Cataloging in Publication Data

Rankin, William Parkman.
    Business management of general consumer maga-
zines.

    Expansion of doctoral dissertation, New York
University.
    Bibliography: p.
    Includes index.
    1. Periodicals, Publishing of—United States—
Management—Case studies. I. Title.
Z479.R35   070.5'72'0973   80-12147
ISBN 0-03-056696-7

Published in 1980 by Praeger Publishers
CBS Educational and Professional Publishing
A Division of CBS, Inc.
521 Fifth Avenue, New York, New York 10017 U.S.A.

©1980 by Praeger Publishers

0123456789   038   987654321

Printed in the United States of America

to Ruth

FOREWORD

by Peter A. Derow

A free press is critical to a free society, but only a financially strong and independent press has the foundation from which to exercise its role. As my friend Perk Rankin has written, "editorial excellence alone is not sufficient for a publication's health or survival . . . innovative business management is an essential commitment to its success."

The magazine (from the French, *magasin*, or storehouse) has come a long way since 1741 when, within days of each other, Benjamin Franklin and Andrew Bradford published America's first two magazines. Virtually every aspect of magazine publishing has changed since then. One of the most significant changes has been the growing importance of effective business management which, ultimately, spells success or failure for a magazine. The time when a magazine could survive—indeed prosper—with a great editor and good fortune alone has long since past.

In this much needed book Rankin examines the founding, fortunes, successes, and failures of five general interest magazines; two of which made it (happily, *Newsweek* is one of them), and three, for a variety of reasons, which did not. Rankin goes beyond the hows and, supported by considerable research and in many cases firsthand interviews with the participants, spells out the whys as well. It is truly a pioneering study.

This book is fascinating reading for one like myself who has spent his working life in magazine publishing. For students who are considering entering the field, this book will be required reading.

Perk Rankin brings 40 years of wisdom, experience, and acute observation to his study of the business management of general interest magazines. During his career he has spent much of his time patiently sharing his insights with colleagues. Now, students of all ages can benefit from Perk's insights into the challenging, exciting world of magazines.

Peter A. Derow
chairman of the board and president
NEWSWEEK, INC.

PREFACE

Until now the subject of business management in the general magazine field has been virtually neglected by both universities and students aspiring to journalism careers. A recent pilot investigation surveying 150 heads of schools of journalism throughout the United States, yielding 53 responses, reported that no such studies were available at their institutions. Similarly there seems to be an obvious lack of useful background information on the subject among many in today's publishing field.

Hence this book, an expansion of my doctoral dissertation at New York University, which explores in depth the business management aspect of magazine publishing, was written not only for the journalism and business students at both undergraduate and graduate levels, but for business and editorial staff members of general magazines and advertiser and agency executives as well—all who seek a better understanding in this intricate area that encompasses general consumer magazines edited for the lay public.

In these pages I combine my own 40 years of experience in the business vineyards of general magazines (and newspapers) representing five different corporations with an intense three-year study that included personal interviews with scores of experts in both the historical and modern aspects of the business, research reports of publishing companies, all of the trade journals, and various libraries. Never before, to my knowledge, has so much information been brought to bear on this aspect of the publishing business.

To help the reader develop a clearer understanding of both the power and the perishability of the magazine product and to develop sound guidance and direction for their own careers, a good portion of the book concentrates on a detailed analysis of the business history of five prominent magazines, two of which proved to be highly successful and three of which failed as business enterprises. Lessons learned from a study of the business techniques of the early magazine publishers and a comparison of the case histories of techniques and innovations of modern-day publishers should be of tangible benefit in rounding out full awareness and understanding of the management side of the magazine business.

For their valuable contributions to the content of this book I am indebted to scores of persons both in the academic arena, including the deans and chairmen of the many schools of journalism who suggested the need for the book, and in the world of publishing, with special gratitude to the following:

Professors Padmakar M. Sapre, Janice L. Gorn, and Alfred Gross, of New York University; Herbert D. Maneloveg, senior vice-president, Della Femina, Travisano & Partners, Inc.; Stephen E. Kelly, former publisher of the *Saturday Evening Post*; from *Better Homes and Gardens*: Jack D. Rehm, publisher, Robert A. Burnett, president, Otto G. Schaefer, former New York advertising director, Hugh Curley, research director, W. F. Jones, former New York advertising director, and Kenneth P. Zosel, administrative manager; from *Newsweek*: Gibson McCabe, former president, Malcolm Muir, former president, Peter A. Derow, chairman and president, F. E. Davis, senior vice-president, Benjamin Bradlee, editor of the *Washington Post* and former Washington bureau chief of *Newsweek*, and Frederick Beebe, former chairman; from *Life*: Jerome S. Hardy, former publisher, and Andrew Heiskell, chairman; from *This Week*: Euclid M. Covington, former chairman, Ben G. Wright, former chairman and president, John C. Sterling, former chairman, William I. Nichols, former publisher, Raymond A. Helsel, former marketing director, and John R. O'Connor, former vice-president.

I also wish to express my gratitude to several others who helped steer the manuscript toward the press: Dr. Julio Torres, Jr. who helped in the editing of the original writing, Arthur Bellaire, president of Arthur Bellaire, Inc. whose guidance and advice were appreciated, Gene Waggaman, manager of marketing activities of *Newsweek*, whose ideas and encouragement were invaluable, and Ted Slate, library director of *Newsweek* and his staff who were most helpful.

Special gratitude is hereby extended to my wife of 37 years, Ruth Gerard Rankin, for showing unusual forbearance and tolerance during the whole task and offering constructive criticism and unique assistance in the preparation of the book.

CONTENTS

BUSINESS MANAGEMENT of GENERAL CONSUMER MAGAZINES

1

INTRODUCTION

The word magazine is derived from the French *magasin*, the Italian *magazzino* and the Arabic *makhazin*, meaning storehouse. It was simple in later years to describe magazines as storehouses of information.[1]

Alexander Pope, in one of his notes to *Dunciad*, defined magazines in 1743 as "... upstart collections of dullness, folly and so on."[2] Throughout the eighteenth century, news gathering and reporting were so little developed that almost any newspaper might have passed as a magazine by a mere change in format.[3]

In 1794 there were only five magazines in the United States. By 1800 the number had increased to 12, by 1810 there were 40, and by 1825 almost 100. Many of the subscribers to early American magazines considered themselves patrons of these ventures in publishing. George Washington showed concern for their success when he wrote to Mathew Carey in 1788, "I consider such easy vehicles of knowledge more happily calculated than any other, to preserve the liberty, stimulate the industry and meliorate the morals of an enlightened and free people."[4]

In 1740 there evolved a contest to determine who would publish the first magazine in the United States. In November 1740, Benjamin Franklin planned to publish *The General Magazine, and Historical Chronicle, for all the British Plantations in America.* Word of the idea reached Andrew Bradford, son of Pennsylvania's first printer, through John Webbe, a disloyal editor and lawyer. Bradford immediately announced a magazine of his own and on February 13, 1741, published the first issue of his *American Magazine*. Not to be outdone, three days later Franklin published the first issue of the *General Magazine*. It contained 75 pages, twice as many as Bradford's and sold for sixpence sterling. There were no subscribers, only single copy sales.[5]

In early magazine publishing, advertising was in its infancy, and brief advertisements occasionally placed on covers, in supplements, or on the inside pages, brought negligible income. At most, a precarious living wage was the early magazine publisher's reward.

Magazines have many characteristics that set them apart from other print media, and which equip them for important tasks in a democratic society: detecting and reporting the problems that confront it, analyzing and interpreting them, and proposing and weighing alternative solutions. They are not restricted to a narrow geographical area, thereby drawing their readers from all areas. This circulation uniqueness enables them to appeal to highly selective audiences or to broad-based ones. They can give highly specialized treatment to highly specialized subjects, or they can provide a national perspective even to local concerns.[6]

As one observes magazines from the late nineteenth century down to 1975, one cannot help but be impressed by the ways in which, as a whole, they have responded to the varying needs, wants, interests, and concerns of the various segments of American society.

The major consumer magazines began to develop, in an economic sense, as market conditions expanded both for them and for the goods advertised in their pages during the first half of the twentieth century. Other contributory factors to the financial growth and success of consumer magazines were the rise in population, the increase in industrial progress, and the growth of general education.

This book traces the evolution of the business management of selected general consumer magazines in the United States from 1900 through 1975. The subordinate aspects researched included:

1. What was the business management status of selected general consumer magazines in the year 1900?

2. What have been the major improved techniques of effective business management instituted in selected general consumer magazines since 1900?

3. What implications for business education may be derived from the findings of subproblems 1 and 2?

Business Management: Business management in broad terms includes the determination of policy and coordination of functions (administration); the execution of policy and employment of organization (management proper); and the process of combining the work of individuals or groups with the faculties necessary for its execution (organization).[7]

For the purpose of this book the author focused on four aspects of business management: 1) method of operation, 2) structural organization, 3) decision making, and 4) financial control.

General Consumer Magazines: These are nationally circulated magazines that include editorial material that reaches peoples' personal life and interests. The criteria set by the Magazine Committee of the Association of National Advertisers were used for identifying the magazines. These criteria were a minimum circulation of 300,000 and a minimum advertising revenue of $2 million. These figures were verified from the Audit Bureau and the Publishers Information Bureau,[8] respectively.

This book is limited to selected general consumer magazines published in the United States during the years 1900 to 1975.

The year 1900 was a logical starting point for a business management historical analysis of the consumer national magazine. As Theodore Peterson pointed out:

> After 1900, magazine publishing was profoundly affected by changes in the American economy, particularly those in the distribution of consumer goods which led to the growth of advertising. As advertising grew it made the magazine a part of the system of marketing in the United States. This development had manifold effects on the magazine industry. It transformed the publisher from dealer in editorial wares to dealer in consumer groups as well.[9]

The book traces the evolution of the business management aspects of selected magazines from the nine groupings as defined by the Magazine Committee of the Association of National Advertisers: 1) General Weeklies, 2) News, 3) General Monthlies, 4) Mens' and Boys', 5) Outdoor, 6) Sports, 7) Women's Fashion, 8) Home, and 9) syndicated Sunday Supplements.

Trade, technical, scientific, and professional journals were not covered. Also excluded were farm magazines, house organs, fraternal, and organizational magazines.

For over 50 years schools of journalism have been stressing the training of students for editorial positions in the communications field.[10] There is evidence that the business management side of journalism has been neglected by these institutions. Journalism executive Robert McCord charged educators, "You are teaching and we are hiring business dumdums."[11]

To determine further if an investigation into the proposed

subject was expedient, the author wrote to 150 deans or chairpersons of leading schools and departments of journalism throughout the country inquiring as to whether any studies had been undertaken at their schools on the business side of journalism. Fifty-three replies were received. All of the respondents indicated that, to their knowledge, there were no business journalism studies available at their schools, and many added that there was a need for such a study. This thought was exemplified by Loyal Gould:

> I am sorry to report that I am unable to find anything in our university on the business side of journalism. Also, I feel that this is an area all too neglected by academics throughout American universities. . . . We need the type of investigation you seem to be proposing.[12]

Sound management is as essential to the magazine business as it is to any other business. Magazines conform to the usual patterns of all American business. Ownership is usually in the form of individual proprietorship, partnership, or the corporation. A book concerning the many facets of the business management side of magazines should open up a whole new vista of pertinent data useful to those aspiring to a career in the business area of journalism.

As Roland E. Wolseley explained it:

> Because journalism signifies only an editorial activity to many persons, it sometimes comes as a shock to them to find out that in the United States this occupation is an intimate part of the entire business system of the nation. Nor is it merely a part; it also is heavily dependent upon that complex engine.[13]

This book is organized into ten chapters. In Chapter 2, the related literature is reviewed under three categories. The overall research design and the instruments and procedures used in compiling data for the three subproblems are described in Chapter 3. The economic development of early magazines is traced in Chapter 4.

The next five chapters are devoted to a review, in case-history style, of five leading consumer magazines, revealing important aspects of their business management. The last chapter contains a summary of the findings, conclusions by the author, and suggestions for further work.

NOTES

1. Calvin Ellsworth Chunn, "History of News Magazines" (Ph.D. diss., University of Missouri, 1950), p. 2.

2. Frank Luther Mott, *A History of American Magazines*, 5 vols. (Cambridge: Harvard University Press, 1958), vol. 1, pp. 1, 6.

3. Ibid., p. 8.

4. Frank Luther Mott, *American Journalism* (New York: Macmillan, 1941), p. 120.

5. James Playsted Wood, *Magazines in the United States*, 2nd ed. (New York: The Random Press Company, 1956), p. 10.

6. Testimony of Dean Theodore Paterson, University of Illinois, College of Communications, before the United States Postal Rate Commission, Washington, D.C., June 3, 1971.

7. Harold Koontz and Cyril O'Donnell, *Principles of Management* (New York: McGraw-Hill Book Company, Inc., 1959), p. 31.

8. *Magazine Circulation and Rate Trends, 1940-1974* (New York: Association of National Advertisers, Magazine Committee, 1976), p. 1.

9. Theodore Peterson, *Magazines in the Twentieth Century*, 2nd ed. (Urbana: University of Illinois Press, 1964), p. 18.

10. Wesley C. Clark, *Journalism Tomorrow* (Syracuse: Syracuse University Press, 1958), p. v.

11. Robert McCord, executive editor, *Arkansas Democrat* (Little Rock), speaking before the Association for Education in Journalism, Convention Hall, Ottawa, Canada, August 18, 1975.

12. Letter from Loyal Gould, chairman, Department of Journalism, Baylor University, Waco, Texas, August 31, 1976.

13. Roland E. Wolseley, *Understanding Magazines*, 2nd ed. (Ames: The Iowa State University Press, 1969), p. 43.

2

RELATED LITERATURE

The pertinent literature, reviewed in this section, includes the following topics: 1) early history of magazine publishing (1741-1930), 2) modern history of magazine publishing (1930-1975), and 3) business management and economic performance of selected general magazines.

THE EARLY HISTORY OF MAGAZINE PUBLISHING

Lyon Normal Richardson was the first scholar to write an historical treatise on magazines.[1] His study, developed in 1927, traced the history of American magazines during the years 1741-1789, from the time the first two magazines appeared in this country through the year of George Washington's election to the presidency. Richardson included 37 periodicals in his work and listed the distinguished publishers attracted to establishing magazines. Among them were Benjamin Franklin, Andrew Bradford, Jeremy Gridley, Thomas Prince, Jr., William Livingston, William Smith, Noah Webster, Thomas Coke, and Mathew Carey.

It was an economically arduous task to continue publication of a magazine in the middle of the eighteenth century because the publishers depended on subscription lists for support, with very little income from advertising. These subscription lists averaged around 500 and occasionally went to 1,600.

Theodore Bernard Peterson's work[2] on consumer magazines in the United States, 1900-1950, is closely allied to this research, as he touched on the economic history of consumer magazines during that period. He emphasized how advertisers, through the Audit Bureau of Circulations, were a major force in changing the attitude of magazine publishers toward circulation.

He traced the economy of the United States as it made the transition from an agrarian to an industrial state. The magazine audience was widened by population growth, and there was an expanded market both for magazines and the goods advertised in their pages. Magazines of mammoth circulation became commonplace after World War I.

James Playsted Wood reviewed the early history of magazines from 1741, when Benjamin Franklin announced his plans to publish the *General Magazine*, to the year 1955, when the *Saturday Evening Post* appeared in new type and layout.[3] He stressed the magazines' roles as national educators and as literary and crusading forces. He pointed out that the vast improvements in the appearance of modern-day magazines were due to the rise in advertising revenue and better printing, and in the reproductions of illustrations. More efficient methods of magazine distribution also contributed.

One of the most comprehensive studies in the field of general consumer magazines was done by Calvin Ellsworth Chunn in 1950.[4] He set out to do a history of news magazines. However, he began by surveying the history of general consumer magazines, starting in 1741. He chronicled the events leading up to the publication, in 1855, of the first news magazine, *Leslie's Weekly*, and traced the characteristics of the magazines that followed, dwelling more on editorial style and content than on commercial matters. His early historical chronology was helpful as background material for this study.

The first of Frank Luther Mott's five volumes on the history of American magazines contains a wealth of information on the early publications, covering the period from 1741 to 1850.[5] He claimed that magazines offered their reading public "democratic literature" which was sometimes of high quality and appealed to the masses. Again it was emphasized that subscription receipts were almost the sole means of income from magazines. Advertising occasionally appeared in the text pages. Books and pamphlets were the chief items advertised. The first American magazine advertisement, according to Mott, was a reading notice about a ferry, which appeared in Franklin's *General Magazine*, dated May 10, 1741.

THE MODERN HISTORY OF MAGAZINE PUBLISHING

Roland E. Wolseley has done a comprehensive survey of magazine publishing.[6] His work is an overview of modern magazines, and he also analyzed their historical backgrounds. Among the business management points covered, he stressed advertising, ownership, circulation, production, personnel, public relations, and research. He believed changes in the economy were among the causes of the death of some leading magazines. However, as some died, others were born. In 1967 and 1968, when he was writing, he claimed there were 16,000 magazines published monthly in the United States. They developed as transportation and business expanded, and he held that the future of the magazine publishing business might well lie in specialized magazines. He indicated that magazines reached their peak during the first half of the twentieth century in number of publications, persons employed therein, circulation distribution, and advertising revenue.

John Tebbel stated that general consumer magazines were always in a struggle to stay alive, although they survived violent financial swings.[7] Competition for the readers' time was increasing. First, there was the bicycle fad, then automobiles, followed by motion pictures. Radio hurt the most. It was in the home. Magazines that died during this period included *Century*, *St. Nicholas*, *Judge*, *The Delineator*, *North American Review*, *Living Age*, and *Forum Independent*. Two long-established popular magazines, *Harper's Weekly*, begun in 1857, and *The Outlook*, first published in 1867, also died. The publishers would not alter old formulas, and there was strong competition from innovators such as DeWitt Wallace of the *Reader's Digest*, Henry Luce of Time Inc., and Harold Ross of the *New Yorker*. The most interesting phenomenon to many scholars of the years just before and after the turn of the century was the rise and momentary triumph of the ten-cent magazine.

Frank Luther Mott concentrated on a general discussion of magazine publications in the period of 1905-1930. His work included 31 historical sketches of selected magazines.[8] Among them were *Good Housekeeping* and *Better Homes and Gardens*. Edwin Thomas Meredith had started *Fruit, Garden and Home*. It was the forerunner of *Better Homes and Gardens* and was first published in August 1924. During the years of World War I, magazines experienced the first drop in advertising volume, especially food advertising. Immediately after the war, vigorous efforts on the part of publishers centered largely on techniques of cooperation with dealers in construction materials, department stores, and house furnishings.

Jane Grant concluded that three men who changed the whole face of American magazine publishing in the 1920s were Luce, Wallace, and Ross.[9] There were birth pangs, finances were precarious, and it was far from easy for Ross to start the *New Yorker* in the summer of 1925. Others built empires, but Ross never lost sight of his true love: the magazine—the little weekly.

Karyl Van's and John Hahn's interest was advertising and its effect on magazine publishing.[10] The advertising sales departments of consumer magazines are well equipped with sales material. Much of it is derived from syndicated data, such as audience studies from Daniel Starch, W. R. Simmons, and Associates Research, Inc.

The publisher, advertising director, advertising manager, or regional manager (depending upon the organization of the company) lead the advertising sales staff in their sales procedures. A number of magazines have marketing departments or divisions which account for the behind-the-scenes preparatory promotional and sales aids so necessary to a successful sales operation.

Robert T. Elson detailed the growth of the magazine publishing empire, Time Inc.[11] In February 1923, two young Yale graduates, Briton Hadden and Henry Robinson Luce, published a 28-page magazine titled *Time*, with a beginning circulation of 9,000. From this small venture grew a world-encircling communications empire. Luce directed the opening of corporate records so that this history could be authoritative and complete. Another related analysis was James L. C. Ford's comprehensive study of specialized publications,[12] a multimillion dollar business that affects the entire economy of the United States. All specialized magazines were covered except mass circulation publications such as *Life*, *Reader's Digest*, and *Look*.

Investigation of the attitudes of journalism executives toward the various types of educational backgrounds and the experience desirable for employees in the broadcast industry is offered by Leon Higbee in tangentially related research to this book.[13] He used the normative-survey technique through mail questionnaires to a random sample of 310 broadcast executives who are representative of the 1,709 executives in eight Rocky Mountain states. Among the findings were:

1. Nearly three-fourths of the respondents believed a college degree essential. They also believed a broad liberal college education was more important than learning specific broadcasting skills.

2. Nearly half of the respondents (48.5 percent) recommended a four-year college degree program combined with on-the-job training.

3. A majority of respondents believed that many television-radio courses are too theoretical to be of real value to the student.

The need for closer cooperation and better understanding between journalism executives and educators was obvious from the findings of Higbee's study.

Research in an allied field was done by Gerald Cory Stone on the management of resources in community-sized newspapers.[14] Revenues and costs of operation of newspapers were investigated, as well as the management structure and the differences in the backgrounds of the publishers involved. He concluded that financial success of community newspapers is determined by flexible internal management decisions, rather than the inflexible conditions of the community of publication. Due to the fact that community newspaper's content is stable, and because key aspects of the annual financial statements are highly interrelated, it is possible to predict annual adjusted gross income, total annual expenses, and net income of the newspaper by counting the inches of advertising copy in two consecutive issues of the newspaper.

Roland E. Wolseley reviewed the major problems besetting magazine publishers and management, including increases in postal rates, competition from other media, and the rise in labor costs.[15] He stated that magazines continue to be an important medium of mass communication despite certain gloomy predictions following the demise of the *Saturday Evening Post, Look,* and *Life.*

Wolseley further stated that because advertising is essential to business in general, and magazines offer access to specialized marketplaces, too expensive to find and reach any other way, magazines will continue to grow and prosper. In 1958 he predicted that magazine management would emphasize specialized subject magazines rather than mass-circulation periodicals.

A comprehensive study of the syndicated Sunday magazine field was undertaken by John Arberry Haney in the early 1950s.[16]

Inventions such as higher speed presses, allowing less-expensive printing, and better picture reproduction made mass-syndicated Sunday magazines possible. At first the value of the Sunday magazine lay in its power to increase Sunday newspaper circulation. Later, it was discovered to be a valuable advertising medium. By 1924 the magazine *American Weekly* was estimated to be returning approximately $2 million a year in profit to the Hearst Corporation.

BUSINESS MANAGEMENT AND THE ECONOMIC PERFORMANCE OF SELECTED GENERAL MAGAZINES

Peter Drucker[17] examined the techniques of effective business management and attempted to identify the new knowledge needed, the new challenges business faces, and the new tasks ahead.

Drucker stated, "But what is it to manage a business? What management is supposed to do, and how it should be doing it, are subjects which are rarely discussed."[18] In this study it is necessary to discuss important management functions when analyzing each selected consumer magazine. As Drucker reiterated, "There is only one valid definition of business purpose: to create a customer." [19]

Edward Mason presented a collection of analyzed data on the thinking of leading educators in the fields of law, economics, business, political science, and social research that was of assistance to the researcher as background information.[20] One precept covered was that market power and managerial power reinforce each other in complex ways. In the researcher's investigation of the managerial operation of selected consumer magazines the problem of power was encountered in several areas, especially among the larger magazines. As Mason approached the subject, he pointed out that legitimacy is a problem, mainly because of the existence of private power. Power, he maintains, is a tricky concept, and is even trickier to measure. There is a useful distinction between power to do (that is, capability) and power over, which is anathema.

A study closely allied to the objectives of the present one was conducted by Donald Wayne Jugenheimer.[21] The purpose of his study was to examine, evaluate, and predict the numbers and types of new mass media and to determine the advertising usage of advanced communications technologies. The study involved a thorough search of printed material dealing with predictions of future communications technology. The final conclusion was that fewer media, and more similar types of media, will complicate advertising media evaluation and selection procedures. The eventual outcome of these developments will be more simplified, diverse, and flexible media selection for advertising.

A field of study that was appropriate as related literature was conducted by Mort P. Stern.[22] He was a "participant observer," which requires both involvement and detachment. He was both doctoral candidate researcher and an executive of the *Denver Post*. Stern claimed that researchers in human organizations answer the questions of objectivity by stating that this problem can be overcome by the attitude of the researcher and the methods used in reporting data. Stern's study, in addition to its utility as an in-depth inquiry, contains much data of value to the author of an historical journalism nature not available in other sources.

Deborah Baldwin's thesis provided some background information.[23] She traced the late history of the *Saturday Review* magazine, starting in 1940 when Norman Cousins assumed the editorship until November 1971, when he resigned. The magazine was taken over by two young entrepreneurs, named Nicholas Charney and John Veronis, who hoped to use the magazine corpse as a cornerstone in the communications empire. In October 1972, they divided up the remains of *Saturday Review* into four monthlies, all with the prefix *Saturday Review*. This bold move failed, and after their last futile attempt at refinancing in April 1973, Norman Cousins bought back the name and mailing lists in July 1973 for $500,000 and combined it with *World* to form a single biweekly, which he named *Saturday Review/World*.

An important element in the analysis of the business operation of the selected consumer magazines in this book was the decision-making process. According to Peter F. Drucker, the effective decision maker always tries to put his solution on the highest possible conceptual level. His decision has to be adequate and within boundary conditions. It needs to be adequate to its purpose. This setting of boundaries and conditions cannot be done on facts alone, but always has to be done on interpretation. It is a risk-taking judgment. Decisions that do not satisfy boundary conditions may be ineffectual and inappropriate.[24]

Auren Uris found that the method of operation of a business has many facets and that new knowledge must be blended with traditional wisdom. He suggested:

> That managers must be able to analyze their working problems, solve them in practical, realistic fashion, and organize their energies effectively to cope with job routines and problems with reasonable timeliness.[25]

Uris points out that the earliest business executives, as well as the early magazine publishers, were entrepreneurs. They became top administrators because, in many cases, they started the business, put up the capital, and assumed the risks. As they needed additional managers, typically, they brought in family members or friends. The family business continued into the late decades of the nineteenth century. By the 1950s the number of privately owned corporations had declined substantially. Closely owned corporations usually reached a point beyond which they could not grow. Competing firms run by professionals were soon able to pass them by.[26]

Bertram M. Gross extended the above theory and wrote that at a more specific level of management we find processes such as planning, activating, and evaluating. Each involves decision making and communication. Each is part of a "seamless web" of organization. Technical processes involved include production management, accounting, budgeting and finance, operations research, personnel management, and marketing. These administrative processes are the central concern of administrative rationality.[27]

"A business is a collection of resources committed by an individual or group of individuals, who hope that the investment will increase in value,"[28] according to Walter B. Meigs, Charles E. Johnson, and A. N. Nosich. Financial accounting is an essential process in the operation of any business and, in particular, magazine publishing. Interpretation and analysis of financial information is not the sole province of the accountant. Managers, investors, and creditors must make effective use of accounting information in order for a business to succeed.

In many of the early magazines in the United States accounting records were kept for a single proprietorship and did not include accounts for capital stock, retained earnings, or dividends. The capital account was usually credited with the amount of the proprietor's original investment and also with any subsequent investments made in the company.[29]

Structural organization is the most detailed and perhaps the most difficult part of organizing, especially in deciding on the content of the various executive positions and determining how to group them under top management at various levels. Ernest Dale[30] strongly suggests that circumstances must govern in structuring jobs and grouping them at various levels. As businesses grow larger, various executives within the organization must be given instructions on:

1. The objectives of the whole organization . . . and the part he is expected to play in reaching it.
2. Whom he has line authority over, and who has line authority over him.
3. His relationship with others on his own level .
4. The deadlines it is necessary to observe if other segments of the organization are to meet their objectives.[31]

NOTES

1. Lyon Norman Richardson, *A History of Early American Magazines, 1741-1789* (New York: Thomas Nelson & Sons, 1931).

2. Theodore Bernard Peterson, "Consumer Magazines in the United States, 1900-1950, A Social and Economic History" (Ph.D. diss., University of Illinois, 1955).

3. James Playsted Wood, *Magazines in the United States* (New York: The Ronald Press Company, 1956).

4. Calvin Ellsworth Chunn, "History of News Magazines" (Ph.D. diss., University of Missouri, 1950).

5. Frank Luther Mott, *A History of American Magazines*, 5 vols. (Cambridge: Harvard University Press, 1958), vol. 1, p. 1.

6. Roland E. Wolseley, *Understanding Magazines*, 2nd ed. (Ames: The Iowa State University Press, 1969).

7. John Tebbel, *The American Magazine, A Compact History* (New York: Hawthorn Books, Inc., 1969).

8. Mott, *History*, vol. 5.

9. Jane Grant, *Ross, The New Yorker and Me* (New York: Reynal and Company, 1968).

10. Karyl Van and John Hahn, *Guidelines in Selling Magazine Advertising* (New York: Meredith Corporation, 1971).

11. Robert T. Elson, *Time Inc.* (New York: Atheneum, 1968).

12. James L. C. Ford, *Magazines for Millions* (Carbondale: Southern Illinois University Press, 1969).

13. Arthur Leon Higbee, "A Survey of the Attitudes of Selected Radio and Television Broadcast Executives toward the Educational Background and Experience Desirable for Broadcast Employees" (Ph.D. diss., Michigan State University, 1970).

14. Gerald Cory Stone, "Management of Resources in Community-Sized Newspapers" (Ph.D. diss., Syracuse University, 1975).

15. Roland E. Wolseley, *The Changing Magazine* (New York: Hastings House, 1973).

16. John Arberry Haney, "A History of the Nationally Syndicated Sunday Magazine Supplements" (Ph.D. diss., University of Missouri, 1953).

17. Peter Drucker, *Management* (New York: Harper & Row, 1974).

18. Ibid., p. 50.

19. Ibid., p. 61.

20. Edward S. Mason, *The Corporation in Modern Society* (Cambridge: Harvard University Press, 1961).

21. Donald Wayne Jugenheimer, "Future Communications Technology Advances and Their Principal Implications for Advertising" (Ph.D. diss., University of Illinois, 1972).

22. Mort. P. Stern, "Palmer Hoyt and the *Denver Post*" (Ph.D. diss., University of Denver, 1969).

23. Deborah Baldwin, "The Demise of the *Saturday Review*" (Master's thesis, University of Oregon, 1974).

24. Peter F. Drucker, *The Effective Executive* (New York: Harper & Row, 1967), pp. 128, 130, 131.

25. Auren Uris, *Mastery of Management* (Homewood, Ill.: Dow Jones-Irwin, Inc., 1968), p. 24.

26. Ibid., p. 48.

27. Bertram M. Gross, *Organizations and their Managing* (New York: Macmillan Publishing Company Inc., 1964), pp. 45-46.

28. Walter B. Meigs, Charles E. Johnson, and A. N. Nosich, *Financial Accounting* (New York: McGraw-Hill Book Company, 1970), p. 5.

29. Ibid., p. 199.

30. Ernest Dale, *Organization* (New York: American Management Association, 1967), p. 140.

31. Ibid.

3

RESEARCH METHOD AND INSTRUMENTATION

The logic of historical thought is not always the product of a formal logic of deductive inference, nor is it always an inductive logic, similar to that of John Stuart Mill or John Maynard Keynes. The answers may be general or particular. History is a problem-solving discipline.[1]

The author incorporated the procedures suggested by Louis Gottschalk for the writing of history:

> The process of critically examining and analyzing the record and survivals of the past is here called historical method. The imaginative reconstruction of the past from the data derived by that process is called historiography (the writing of history). By means of historical method and historiography (both of which are frequently grouped together simply as historical method) the historian endeavors to reconstruct as much of the past of mankind as he can.[2]

Other principles of historical research that were examined and adhered to included those discussed by Allan Nevins,[3] Jacques Barzun and Henry F. Graff,[4] and David H. Fischer.[5] Nevins claimed that a knowledge of history is needed in order to throw the present into perspective. He stated that, "The most important part of history is really a series of problems, and more than half of the historian's work is to make a statement of attempted solutions."[6]

Barzun and Graff outlined important virtues of historical writing. These included accuracy, as facts must be ascertained. Next was "love of order." One must have a system which keeps order. Also essential is orderliness which implies logic, and honesty because one must be a searcher after truth. Self-awareness is important because it lessens the influence of bias, and lastly, imagination, whereby researchers must imagine the kind of source they would like to have before they can find it.

Fischer advocated a careful process of selection. The various processes of selection should be clarified if history is to develop. The determination of fundamental criteria of factual significance is involved in this problem, and all historians must operate upon certain criteria of factual significance in their work.

Secondary source material was used when appropriate throughout the book.

All source material was subjected to both external and internal criticism to insure its genuineness and validity.

External and low criticism requires an examination of documents to establish the authenticity of the origin of the data.[7]

Internal or high criticism is concerned with the meaning and trustworthiness of statements within the document in question after its authenticity has been established.[8] Some questions which the author asked in order to determine external authenticity were:[9]

1. Is the relic or document a true one rather than a forgery, a counterfeit, or a hoax?
2. Is the document an original version or a copy?
3. Has the age or authorship been firmly established?
4. Are these elements consistent with known facts about the person, the knowledge available, and the technology of the period in which the remains or document originated?

Questions which the author applied to determine internal validity were:[10]

1. Although it may be genuine, does it reveal a true picture?
2. What of the writer or creator? Was he or she competent, honest, unbiased, and actually acquainted with the facts?
3. Did he or she make a record of the testimony, and was he or she able to remember accurately what happened?

The above procedures were applied appropriately to each subproblem.

SUBPROBLEM 1

What was the business management status of selected general consumer magazines in the year 1900?

The author collected both primary and secondary sources of information.* Primary source material was sought at the publishing headquarters of the magazines selected for the study. Such material included minutes of meetings and historical records in the library files. Each magazine publishing enterprise selected for the study had an extensive library facility. As the result of personal contacts developed over many years by the author, it was possible for him to have access to these library files. Important examples of secondary source material were found in the following works:† Frederick Lewis Allen, *Only Yesterday: An Informal History of the Twenties*; Willard Grosvenor Bleyer, *Main Currents in the History of American Journalism*; Frank Luther Mott, *A History of American Magazines*, 5 vols.; Lyon Norman Richardson, *A History of Early American Magazines, 1741-1789*; John Tebbel, *The American Magazine, A Compact History*; James Playsted Wood, *Magazines in the United States*; Theodore Peterson, *Magazines in the Twentieth Century*; and Roland E. Wolseley, *Understanding Magazines*.

Answers to the following questions were sought:

1. What management procedures and new forms of operation were adopted by consumer magazines in the years immediately preceding 1900?

2. What economic conditions profoundly affected the changes in magazine publishing after 1900? How was the sale of magazines expanded? What stimulated the magazine publisher to do research? How did the growth of advertising make magazines a part of the system of marketing in the United States?

3. What were the personal characteristics of the management executives who controlled the business side of these magazines?

The third question listed above is important because, as Allan Nevins wrote: "The history written in the future will necessarily be eclectic in the best sense ... Because even business cannot be interpreted solely by statistics of prices and profits." [11]

Principles of historical research and external and internal criti-

---

*The author was guided by Gottschalk's (*Understanding History*, p. 53) definition of and criteria for use of secondary and primary sources.

†The complete facts of publication for these works are given the first time they are cited in the chapters that follow.

cism, as described previously, were employed in the examination and treatment of the data used in subproblem 1.

SUBPROBLEM 2

What have been the major innovations and improved techniques of effective business management instituted in selected general consumer magazines since 1900?

The sources of data included both primary and secondary information of a biographical, descriptive, and analytical nature related to the management techniques of general consumer magazines studied in the period after 1900.

The aim of the second subproblem was to analyze the major innovations and improved techniques of effective business management in the magazines selected for the study. In effect, this subproblem was a case-by-case study of the selected magazines. This again necessitated personal visits to each of the publishing institutions now in existence. During these visits an attempt was made to examine primary sources, such as company records and board meeting minutes, and to conduct personal interviews with present and past leading business executives of these organizations.

In order to preplan the interviews with these present and former top level executives, the open-ended, focused interview technique was used, employing procedures suggested by Walter Van Dyke Bingham and Bruce Victor Moore [12] and Robert L. Kahn and Charles F. Cannell. [13] The respondents were advised prior to the event concerning the nature and purpose of the interview. An outline* of the questions was supplied during the interview, and the executives were encouraged to expand on the pertinent issues.

Secondary sources were again used as background and supplementary information. Much of this secondary source material was found in magazine publication libraries, the Magazine Publishers Association library, and the libraries of selected schools of journalism.

Secondary sources were sought which outlined the major effective business management processes instituted in selected general consumer magazines since 1900. Some examples of these sources are as follows:

1. *Journalism History*, published quarterly by the California State University, Northridge Foundation, Northridge, California.

---

*For the interview outline, see Appendix A.

2. *Journalism Quarterly*, published quarterly by the Association for Education in Journalism, School of Journalism, Ohio State University, Athens, Ohio.

3. Calvin Ellsworth Chunn, "History of News Magazines," Ph.D. diss., University of Missouri, 1950.

4. Karyl Van and John Hahn, *Guidelines in Selling Magazine Advertising*, New York: Meredith Corporation, 1971.

5. Robert T. Elson, *Time, Inc.*, New York: Atheneum, 1968.

6. John Arberry Haney, "A History of the Nationally Syndicated Sunday Magazine Supplements," Ph.D. diss., University of Missouri, 1953.

7. Lyndon O. Brown, Richard S. Lessler, and William M. Weilbacher, *Advertising Media*, New York: The Ronald Press Company, 1957.

8. *Folio: The Magazine for Magazine Management*, published monthly by Folio Magazine Publishing Corporation, New Canaan, Connecticut.

The following questions were asked in analyzing the data: 1) Did the business executives of the selected general consumer magazines recognize the importance of sound business management in the years following 1900; 2) What were the stated management objectives incorporated in the early magazine operations of the selected general consumer magazines; 3) What evidence is there of the introduction of modern business management techniques among the magazines in the study; and 4) What factors precipitated a recognition of the phenomenon that magazine publishing was inextricably linked with the marketing system?

SUBPROBLEM 3

What implications for business education may be derived from the findings of subproblems 1 and 2?

First, the author analyzed and assessed the performance and accomplishments of the management of selected general consumer magazines up to 1900 as set forth in subproblem 1. Next, he analyzed and assessed the major innovations and the improvements in the techniques of business management since 1900, instituted in the magazines selected for study as disclosed in subproblem 2. Third, he synthesized the data derived in subproblems 1 and 2 and determined their implications for business education in the United States, by posing the following questions: 1) What historical findings relative to the business processes of the magazines selected for the study are useful in determining content of journalism courses? 2) To what extent are the major innovations and improved management techniques adopted by the selected magazines in the study useful as bases of course instruction for students aspiring to careers in magazine business journalism? 3) To what degree do the findings of the study incorporate research data pertinent to business journalism which now appear to be lacking in journalism schools?

NOTES

1. David Hackett Fischer, *Historians' Fallacies* (New York: Harper & Row, 1970), p. xv.

2. Louis Gottschalk, *Understanding History: A Primer of Historical Method*, 2nd ed. (New York: Alfred A. Knopf, Inc., 1969), p. 48.

3. Allan Nevins, *The Gateway to History* (Garden City, N.Y.: Doubleday & Company, 1962), p. 207.

4. Jacques Barzun and Henry F. Graff, *The Modern Researcher*, rev. ed. (New York: Harcourt, Brace & World, Inc., 1970), pp. 58-61.

5. Fischer, *Fallacies*, pp. 64, 65.

6. Nevins, *Gateway*, p. 207.

7. John W. Best, *Research in Education*, 2nd ed. (Englewood Cliffs, N.J.: Prentice-Hall, Inc., 1970), pp. 104-5.

8. Ibid., p. 105

9. Ibid., pp. 104, 105.

10. Ibid., p. 105.

11. Nevins, *Gateway*, p. 17.

12. Walter Van Dyke Bingham and Bruce Victor Moore, *How to Interview*, 4th rev. ed. (New York: Harper & Row, 1959), pp. 71-76.

13. Robert L. Kahn and Charles F. Cannell, *The Dynamics of Interviewing* (New York: John Wiley & Sons, Inc., 1957), pp. 233-52.

4

THE ECONOMIC DEVELOPMENT OF
EARLY MAGAZINES

EIGHTEENTH-CENTURY MAGAZINES

The history of magazines parallels the development of our nation. As in the present, eighteenth-century magazines discussed the problems of the day, which, also like today's, were largely economic in origin. Between 1741 and 1789 three wars were fought which culminated in major political adjustments: 1) King George's War, 2) the French and Indian War, and 3) the Revolutionary War.

The early magazines featured articles on control of taxation, treaties with Indian tribes, security of trade lanes, advancement of industry and commerce, and issuance of currency. The student of fiscal matters alone will find hundreds of pages devoted to the subject.[1]

As recorded previously, these early magazine publishers depended on subscribers for support, and at most, a nominal income was their reward. The normal subscription price was, in the coinage of the day, around a shilling. Most of the magazine publishers also owned newspapers, and these men were usually engaged in several projects in order to extend their fortunes. The cost of postal delivery was slight; the usual practice was for the publisher to make special arrangements with the carriers or to present them with gifts.[2]

During the early eighteenth century there were seven magazines in existence in the United States, and there was a dry spell of ten years, culminated by only three magazine-publishing attempts from 1760 to 1774.[3] But, as today, not all roads lead to Rome. Some lead to

Lethe. Magazines were terminated, and sometimes for reasons other than inadequate support. The demise of *The American Magazine*, a pre-Revolutionary magazine, was explained in a "Postscript" in the magazine's last issue as follows:

> The Proprietors take this opportunity once more to express their grateful sense of the unmerited reception this magazine' has met with from all quarters; which has been such that if reputation or profit had been their motive, the work would have been long continued. But the design was at first set on foot by a number of gentlemen, merely with a view to promote a taste for Letters and useful Knowledge in this American world, and as several of the principal hands who first engaged in it, are now obliged to give their constant attention to other matters, the carrying on of the work falls too heavy on the remainder, so that it has been determined to discontinue it, at least for sometime.[4]

This farewell note was dated November 14, 1758.

EARLY NINETEENTH-CENTURY MAGAZINES

The first magazine to be launched in the nineteenth century in the United States was the *Boston Weekly Magazine* published by Samuel Gilbert and Thomas Dean on October 30, 1802. In 1804 the publishers suffered a serious loss by fire, but friends came to their aid, and they were able to continue to publish until October 1805, when they sold out to Joshua Belcher and Samuel T. Armstrong.[5] There were weekly magazines, sectional magazines, and religious magazines started in the early 1800s, but none was of lasting significance and each changed ownership many times.

North American Review

The *North American Review* was founded in 1815, as a monthly. Its early material was made up of national and international public affairs. The magazine changed its time of publication four times: in 1875 to a quarterly; in 1877 to bimonthly; in 1878 to monthly; and in 1906 back to bimonthly.[6] Though national in coverage, the *Review* never had a large circulation, but soon after its founding it became, and continued to be throughout its existence, a magazine of real power and influence because it was read and studied by the leading men of the country.[7]

In the years following 1825 there was a decided increase in

magazine-publishing activity and the *New York Mirror* called it the golden age of periodicals.[8] John Tebbel labeled the era a turning point in magazine publishing:

> Out of this ferment—and particularly the rapid spread of education, the reduction of illiteracy, the improvements of printing machinery, and the rise of the cities—came the nearly incredible expansion of the magazine business from its modest beginnings to mass market size. America itself was expanding in every direction, but no aspect of it was growing faster than magazines.[9]

Godey's Lady's Book

One of the most important magazines of this period was the famous *Godey's Lady's Book*. It was started in Boston in July 1830, and lasted until August 1898. In the opinion of Fred L. Pattee, a pioneer historian of American literature, the era of the magazine can be said to have begun with this publication.[10] Its publisher was Louis A. Godey, who was known as "two-thirds business man." The circulation of his publication was unusual for this period, reaching 150,000 just before the Civil War.[11] Godey has been considered a most successful magazine publisher, as he left a fortune of $1 million when he died. In 1877, after surviving the Civil War, the management of the magazine, which had been in the hands of Godey's sons, was reorganized, and S. Annie Frost became the chief editor. In 1883 the property was taken over by J. H. Haulenbeck as owner and editor. Its name was changed to *Godey's Magazine* after it was moved to New York City in 1892. In 1898 it was absorbed by Frank Munsey's *Puritan*.[12]

Graham's Magazine

In 1840 George R. Graham began issuing a new periodical which he named *Graham's Magazine*. Mott commented that this magazine "... in the five years 1841-45 displayed a brilliance which has seldom been matched in American magazine history."[13]

LATE NINETEENTH-CENTURY MAGAZINES

Atlantic

The *Atlantic* magazine was founded in Boston in 1857 and was devoted to literature, art, and politics. Later, science was added to its subtitle. It was, in a sense, in competition with New York's *The Galaxy* which began publishing in 1866. This rivalry continued until 1878.[14]

Atlantic never reached large circulation figures, attaining only 50,000 by 1874. It was considered economically unsound and almost disappeared in 1909. However, it was rejuvenated by Ellery Sedgwick and went on to reach five times its highest nineteenth-century circulation by the middle of the twentieth century.[15]

Harper's Bazaar

Magazines started by major publishing houses tended to be more stable, since they had the financial resources of a successful publisher behind them. One such publication was *Harper's Bazaar*, published by Harper & Row, which appeared for the first time in November 1867. It rose to a circulation of 80,000 in its first decade. Its fashion plates were of primary interest along with its English serials, double-page pictures, stories, and splendid art work. The magazine survived many original problems and in 1901 Fletcher Harper looked for a way out. In 1913 the magazine, which had become a monthly, came to the attention of William Randolph Hearst. He bought the magazine for his International Magazine Company, which he was then building. *Harper's Bazaar* thrives today and has become a sophisticated, leading high-fashion magazine.[16]

Saturday Evening Post

In 1897 Cyrus H. K. Curtis bought the *Saturday Evening Post* for $1,000. Subscriptions at that time had dropped to 2,000 each week, and there was virtually no advertising. Curtis hired George Horace Lorimer as editor, and together they succeeded in making the magazine famous as a conservative and commercially successful weekly. In spite of stiff competition from large and flourishing magazines such as *Collier's*, *Leslie's*, and *Harper's Weekly*, it remained a successful publication from the turn of the twentieth century until the 1950s.[17]

Leslie's Weekly

Leslie's Weekly had a successful existence from 1855 to 1922. It stressed news in pictures and in text and, at times, had the typographical appearance of a newspaper. From a circulation standpoint, it was one of the most successful publishing ventures of its century. Its circulation reached 164,000 just before the Civil War, increased briefly to 347,000, and then dropped below 50,000 after the Civil War. Mrs. Leslie attempted to carry on after Frank Leslie's death, but was unsuccessful and sold the magazine. A succession of owners kept it going as a general publication through World War I, and during the early war years its circulation reached 400,000. However, the low economic state of the nation after World War I contributed to *Leslie's* demise, as well as that of other magazines that could not cope with high production costs.[18]

Magazine publishers, just before the turn of the twentieth century, were considering lowering the prices of their publications to insure steady circulation growth. They were encouraged by the success of several magazines, including the *Ladies' Home Journal* which had, by 1893, built up a circulation of 700,000 at ten cents a copy. The depression of the mid-nineties and decreases in costs of printing and paper, as well as the invention of a new technique of photoengraving, known as the halftone, encouraged magazine publishers to lower their copy prices.[19] These early magazines priced at ten cents were causing a revolution in the field of periodical publishing. What did they have besides the attraction of price to make them popular? Mott declared:

> ... What did characterize them were copious and well-printed illustrations, liveliness and freshness in presentation of nonfiction articles, variety in subject matter, a serious treatment of contemporary problems, a keen interest in new inventions and progress in general, and attention of major world events. These magazines had also, we must not forget, the attraction of success; there was a popular appeal in the numbers fat with advertising.[20]

The last decade of the nineteenth century was a happy time for magazines. This era was described by Theodore Peterson as follows:

> As the century turned, the characteristics of the twentieth-century popular magazine were clearly discernible. What were they? First, magazines had become low in price. Their low price, ten cents and even five cents, put them within reach of an increased proportion of the American people.... Before the last decade of the nineteenth century, publishers had been extremely proud of circulations between 100,000 and 200,000; but by 1900, Bok's *Ladies' Home Journal* was moving rapidly toward a circulation of 1,000,000. Advertising, attracted by large circulations as manufacturers

quested for a national market, had become virtually essential for the success of a low-priced magazine.[21]

FIRST HALF OF THE TWENTIETH CENTURY

As the twentieth century began, there was a surge of extraordinary industrial and financial development in the United States. A variety of factors interacted to demonstrate the vitality of the times including the growth of large cities, the progress in the West and South, the immigration problem, new and often radical political movements, the growth of labor organizations, revolutionary inventions in transportation and industry, a shifting emphasis in religion, the emancipation of women, new movements in literature and art and the theatre, and the extraordinary development in education, journalism, sports, and publishing.

These phenomena became more rapidly apparent to contemporary observers because of the improvement in the media of communication. Of all the agencies of popular information, none experienced a more spectacular enlargement and increase in effectiveness than magazines.[22]

National consumer magazines rode a wave of economic cyclical change. They were favored by the times, characterized by the shift from an agrarian to an industrial economy. These conditions were stimuli for magazines of large national circulations. There was a distinct need for a medium which could take the advertiser's message simultaneously to large groups of consumers over a widespread area.[23]

In the first half of the twentieth century not only did the number of magazine readers increase tremendously, but so did the number of magazines. There were a thousand more magazines in the United States in 1950 than in 1900. In a sense, the magazine publisher performed a marketing function, and the fortunes of the magazine industry became closely dependent upon the health of the economy in general.

Munsey's Magazine

Frank Munsey, who first published his *Munsey's Magazine* in 1893, estimated that there were 250,000 magazine purchasers in the United States. He further estimated that the ten-cent magazine had increased the number to 750,000.[24] In 1947, in a nationwide audience study, the Magazine Advertising Bureau reported that there were 32.3 million magazine-reading families.[25]

Ladies' Home Journal

Ladies' Home Journal was the only magazine with a circulation of a million in 1900. By 1950 there were 40 general and farm magazines with circulations of one million or more.[26] The growth of the general magazine industry from 1900 on was the result of an expanding market in this country. The general demand for advertisers' goods and services resulted in more advertising volume for the magazine publishers who became dealers in consumer goods as well as dealers in an editorial product. The magazines in existence in 1900 sold their product at much less than cost and depended on advertising revenue for their profit.

In the decade just prior to 1900 the United States was reaching an economic climax coupled with an increased tempo of life in general, a new international outlook and a need for the dissemination of news. During this period, general magazines were changing to keep pace with the hectic developments. The halftone engraving was perfected; color presses and rotogravure became popular; faster printing presses were manufactured along with quicker typesetting machines and more rapid news transmission.

According to Wood, advertising made possible the popular magazines of the 1880s and the 1890s. National advertising, which originated in magazines, had applied and continues to apply its own powerful leverage in American life. It also played an important role in originating modern methods of distribution and manufactured goods, and has helped bring about a virtual revolution in the production methods employed by American industry, mass selling sustaining mass production.[27]

Business soon recognized the economic power of the force intensified and expanded by general magazines. Chauncey M. Depew, then president of the New York Central and Hudson River Railroad, said, "Every enterprise, every business, and I might add every institution, must be advertised in order to be a success. To talk in any other strain would be madness."[28] In the year 1891 the Pennsylvania Railroad spent $230,000 in advertising, and the Union Pacific almost as much.[29]

Literary Digest and the Pathfinder

Two important news magazines sprang up in this transition period, and their reader interest enabled them to live for many years. The first was the *Literary Digest*, a magazine published by Funk & Wagnalls Company, which supplied excerpts of opinions of the press on certain news of the day. Its first issue appeared on March 1,

1890.[30] The second was the *Pathfinder*, founded by George D. Mitchell and first published in Washington on January 6, 1894. Its slogan was, "A National Newspaper for Young Americans," and its first print order was 25,000 copies. The magazine grew slowly, but after five years showed a profit, and moved into its own building, equipped with its own printing plant.[31]

Successful Farming

Edwin T. Meredith started his career in publishing at the age of 17, working part-time in the mailing room of his grandfather's Populist newspaper, the *Farmer's Tribune*. In 1894 he quit college and took over control of the *Farmer's Tribune*. While working on the newspaper, Meredith began to make plans for the publication of a magazine of interest to farmers. He published the first issue of *Successful Farming* in October 1902.[32]

The magazine was started in three rooms in a building at Fourth and Grand in Des Moines, Iowa. By 1912 the company had expanded several times and all operations were moved to a new plant at 1716 Locust Street where the Meredith Corporation is still located. *Successful Farming* used many circulation and sales promotion schemes to stimulate the growth of the publication, many of which involved the readers in contests as well as subscription sales.[33]

As transportation and business expanded and illiteracy decreased, magazines developed. Advertising directors of magazines were able to solicit advertising among a wide range of business prospects as transportation lines fanned out connecting widely separated communities.

The magazines described were some of the products of what has been called "The Second Golden Age."[34] The magazine business now had quality as well as quantity.

NOTES

1. Lyon N. Richardson, *A History of American Magazines* (New York: Thomas Nelson and Sons, 1931), p. 3.

2. Ibid., p. 3.

3. Frank Luther Mott, *A History of American Magazines*, 5 vols. (Cambridge: Harvard University Press, 1958), vol. 1, p. 26.

4. Richardson, *History*, p. 122.

5. Mott, *History*, vol. 5, p. 247.

6. John E. Drewry, *Some Magazines and Magazine Makers* (Boston: The Stratford Company, 1924), pp. 26, 27.

7. James Playsted Wood, *Magazines in the United States*, 2nd ed. (New York: The Ronald Press Company, pp. 1956), p. 46.

8. *New York Mirror*, November 15, 1828, VI, p. 151.

9. John Tebbel, *The American Magazine* (New York: Hawthorn Books, Inc., 1969), pp. 47-48.

10. Wood, *Magazines*, p. 54.

11. Mott, *History*, vol. 1, p. 581.

12. Ibid., pp. 592, 593.

13. Quoted in Tebbel, *American Magazine*, p. 49.

14. Roland E. Wolseley, *Understanding Magazines*, 2nd ed. (Ames: The Iowa State University Press, 1969), p. 32.

15. Ibid., p. 33.

16. Tebbel, *American Magazine*, p. 124.

17. Ibid., p. 29.

18. Ibid., p. 33.

19. Theodore Peterson, *Magazines in the Twentieth Century*, 2nd ed. (Urbana: University of Illinois Press, 1964), pp. 6, 7.

20. Mott, *History*, vol. 4, pp. 6-7.

21. Peterson, *Magazines*, p. 13.

22. Mott, *History*, vol. 4, p. 2.

23. Peterson, *Magazines*, p. 4.

24. C. C. Regier, *The Era of the Muckrakers* (Chapel Hill: University of North Carolina Press, 1932), p. 20.

25. Magazine Advertising Bureau, *Nationwide Magazine Audience Survey: Report No. 4—Families* (New York: Magazine Advertising Bureau, 1948), p. 12.

26. Edward W. Bok, *A Man from Maine* (New York: Charles Scribner's Sons, 1923), p. 121.

27. Wood, *Magazines*, p. 270.

28. Ernest Elmo Calkins, "Fifty Years of Advertising," *Printers' Ink* (October 10, 1947), p. 26.

29. Wood, *Magazines*, p. 272.

30. Calvin Ellsworth Chunn, "History of News Magazines" (Ph.D. diss., University of Missouri, 1950), p. 289.

31. Ibid., p. 319.

32. Carol Reuss, "*Better Homes and Gardens* and its Editors: An Historical Study from the Magazine's Founding to 1970" (Ph.D. diss., The University of Iowa, 1971), p.8.

33. Ibid., p. 9.

34. Tebbel, *American Magazine*, p. 129.

5

THE SATURDAY EVENING POST

EARLY HISTORY

The magazines described in the previous chapter were enjoying a prosperous time which reached a zenith in the last decade of the nineteenth century. Fortunes were in the making as magazines reached more and more of the American reading public. To trace the emergence of the modern popular magazine one must start with the *Saturday Evening Post*.

It was first published by Charles Alexander and Samuel C. Atkinson on August 4, 1821. Throughout the twentieth century, the Curtis Publishing Company claimed, in a statement reprinted on its masthead cover, that the magazine was founded by Benjamin Franklin in 1728. This claim of antiquity was attributed to Cyrus H. K. Curtis who declared that the *Post* was descended from Franklin's *Pennsylvania Gazette*. However, the *Gazette* ceased publication in 1815, six years before the *Post* was founded.[1]

By 1825 the subscription price of the *Post* was two dollars a year, and advertisements were printed at the rate of three times for one dollar, if they did not exceed a column inch. In 1829 editor Morton McMichael stated that the circulation had reached between 7,000 and 8,000.[2]

During this same year the title of the magazine was changed to *Atkinson's Evening Post, and Philadelphia News* named after the publisher, Samuel Coate Atkinson. In 1840 Atkinson sold the magazine to the firm DuSolle and Graham and a short time later they sold to a company formed by Edmund Deacon and Henry Peterson. The firm finally became H. Peterson & Company which it remained until 1873, when the name was changed to The Saturday Evening Post Company. The magazine itself was retitled the *Saturday Evening Post* and is still called that.[3]

Cyrus H. K. Curtis

In 1897 Cyrus H. K. Curtis bought the magazine from its publisher A. W. Smythe for $1,000. He paid that sum for the name and history alone. At the time, the magazine was a 16-page illustrated weekly, rarely carrying a column of paid advertising.[4] An important contributing factor to the early success of the *Post* was Curtis' choice of George Horace Lorimer as editor. He met Lorimer in Boston, decided he had potential, and hired him as literary editor. After seeing his first four issues, Curtis appointed him editor-in-chief.[5]

> Mr. Curtis had, in high degree, two qualities rare and invaluable in a publisher—the courage to back without limit an idea in which he believed, and a judgment when, having found the right editor, to give that editor a free hand. From that day down to Mr. Curtis' death in 1933, he freely gave Mr. Lorimer the whole power which should accompany responsibility, never interfering directly or indirectly in the editorial content of the *Post*.[6]

Curtis believed that an editor should have business judgment as well as editorial talent, and insisted that his editor write the advertising promotion for the magazine.[7] Lorimer had dictatorial powers and realized the importance of the commercial side of publications. He summed up his belief as follows:

> The conduct of a magazine should be business-like. I never could quite understand why a man should permit the offspring of his brain to be treated as friendless orphans. All writing, up to a certain point, is an artistic matter. But when the manuscript is finished, it becomes, so far as the writer is concerned, a commercial matter too.[8]

The Effect of Advertising

Advertising, to a substantial degree, made possible the low-priced, large-circulation magazine which emerged during the last years of the nineteenth century. One of the leading examples was the *Post*, which effectively demonstrated what soon was to become a basic principle of magazine publishing; namely, that a publisher could lose money on circulation by selling his magazine at less than production cost, yet could reap substantial net profits from advertising revenue.[9] As one publisher of the 1890s remarked: "If I can get a circulation of 400,000 I can afford to give my magazine away to anyone who will pay for the postage."[10]

The Benjamin Franklin Legend

The *Post* was published for more than half a century before it occurred to any of its managers that it might make capital out of the Benjamin Franklin name. Eventually Andrew Smythe, publisher of the *Post* at that time, picked up the idea and advertised in his paper the following, " . . . originally established by Benjamin Franklin in 1728, and appearing in its present character in 1821, it has had an uninterrupted career of 162 years."[11]

The Benjamin Franklin legend was known to have been ready-made for the promotional talents of Cyrus Curtis. As a skilled advertising man and promoter he made the most of it. After his purchase of the *Post* in 1897, never did an issue appear without the name of Franklin as founder. Many historians consider that Benjamin Franklin gave the rejuvenated *Post* something more than a promotional symbol and slogan; he gave it a goal and a standard. Once, in an editorial, the *Post* claimed that when it grew closer to the standard of Benjamin Franklin, it would have circulation of a million.[12]

THE EARLY 1900s

The year 1903 was a good one for the *Post* on both the editorial and business sides, and by the end of 1903 its circulation had passed 600,000.[13] The panic of 1907 slowed its advance somewhat, but the publisher had the foresight to continue a high quality editorial diet. In 1909, the circulation had reached a point of 905,400, and the advertising rate was raised to $3,000 a page.

The increase in circulation and advertising continued until 1913 when the magazine's circulation was more than 2 million a week. Advertising revenue had reached over $5 million in 1910 and was double that in 1914.[14] Building the magazine's annual advertising income from $6,932 in 1897 to almost $100 million in six decades was accomplished, according to *Post* historians, without lowering its high advertising standards.

From its early days the magazine never hesitated to reject advertisements which it considered contrary to its policies or which might be offensive to its readers. In addition to ruling out individual ads which did not meet their standards, Curtis himself put a taboo on three highly profitable general classifications of advertising—liquor, patent-medicine, and financial. For every advertisement in these categories that was kept out, however, two in others seemed to come in.[15]

Two of the interesting phenomena concerning the early success of the *Post* were the independence and the salary of the editor-in-chief during the critical years. George Horace Lorimer held that position from June 10, 1899, when he was appointed by Curtis, to January 1, 1937, a period of 38 years. Just before the Great Depression, starting in 1929, when all Curtis executives took a cut in salary, Lorimer's annual income was reported to be $255,000 a year.[16]

An example of the *Post*'s independence is that, at one time, a powerful group pressed for an article on labor and management and went directly to Curtis. He told them, "You will have to see Mr. Lorimer, the Editor. I am merely the Proprietor."[17]

The Courageous Revival

It appeared for a period of time that maintaining the viability of the magazine would be the most expensive mistake in the annals of American publishing. At one point Curtis cut the price of the *Post* from a dime to a nickel. Public acceptance was still slow so he prodded it with a $250,000 promotional advertising campaign. The *Post* was diving deeper into debt. Circulation was going up but advertising was going down. Soon the deficit reached $800,000. At this point, Curtis told his horrified treasurer that they might as well make the deficit a round figure of $1 million and immediately launched a $200,000 advertising campaign. This was considered to be a demonstration of supreme faith in two things: the *Post* and the power of advertising.[18]

Advertising began to come into the magazine slowly at first, and then as confidence in the publication increased, advertising linage went up. Prudential Insurance Company inserted the first advertisement larger than one-quarter page on February 25, 1899. Quaker Oats took the first two-color advertisement on September 30, 1899. Advertising revenue went from $159,572 in 1900, past the million-dollar mark in 1905, and by 1909 it had trebled to $3,056,402. Two years later it was double that and by 1916 advertising revenue had climbed to $12,089,726 and in 1927, 30 years after Curtis purchased the *Post*, the advertising revenue reached $53,144,987.[19]

The Demise of Cyrus H. K. Curtis

Cyrus Curtis was 70 years old in 1920 and beginning to withdraw from the day-to-day activities of his job. When he was 75 years old he gave 7 percent of the preferred stock as a bonus to the holders of Curtis stock, which was already paying large dividends. Curtis was more than a magazine publisher. He was a civic leader and a public figure and enjoyed his millionaire status. In the public mind he was considered one of the country's great men in the tradition of the poor boy who, through his own efforts, rose to multimillion dollar riches. When he died on June 7, 1933, at the age of 83, he was not just the chairman of the board of the Curtis Publishing Company and the "Man from Maine," as he was known, but he was also a friend of the lowly and the high and mighty. The city of Philadelphia lowered its flags to half staff, tributes were received from Andrew Mellon, Adolph Ochs, the Salvation Army, Jewish charities, publishers of newspapers and magazines, and President Franklin D. Roosevelt.[20] Curtis' will held the trustees to the following policy:

> Believing that the success of the Curtis Publishing Company will be promoted and best insured by the continuance, as far as possible, of the present management and policy, it is my wish and I direct that during the continuance of this trust my common stock of the Curtis Publishing Company shall not be sold unless some extra ordinary contingency shall arise making it desirable to sell, and then only in the event that my trustees unanimously agree.[21]

In effect then, Cyrus Curtis' will forbade the sale of his control of the Curtis Publishing Company.

WEATHERING THE DEPRESSION

The Curtis Publishing Company, which also published the *Ladies' Home Journal, Country Gentleman,* and *Jack and Jill,* reported their 1929 net earnings of $21,534,265, an all-time high for any publishing enterprise. The *Post* was said to have sold $50 million worth of advertising in that year.[22] Even though the financial crash occurred in the late fall of 1929 with its many fiscal casualties, it looked as though the *Post* would weather the storm. Many of the spring issues ran over 200 pages. However, with bank failures across the country and other financial crises, by 1931 advertising had fallen off, and the decline continued through 1932 with some issues only 60 pages in number and advertising down to 12 pages.[23]

The man given the credit for bringing the *Post* advertising through the depths of the Depression was Fred A. Healey. Healey had managed the Chicago office so well that he was made advertising director of the Curtis Publishing Company in 1928. Slowly the advertising volume moved upward and the year 1936 brought great encouragement to Curtis stockholders. The *Post* was able to boast, at the end of that year, that its advertising revenue had amounted to $26,384, 013.[24]

Advertising Growth

The *Post* increased in advertising so rapidly throughout the 1920s that merchants were literally buying up the magazine at five cents as a means of getting inexpensive scrap paper. A monument of sorts was the issue of the *Post* for December 7, 1929. Weighing nearly two pounds, the 272-page magazine contained 20 hours and 20 minutes of reading matter. The 214 national advertisers appearing in that issue paid $1,512,000.[25]

Edward W. Hazen was the advertising director of the Curtis Publishing Company in 1941. Some of the large national advertisers appearing in the *Post* were General Mills, Hartford Fire, Colgate, Gruen, Westinghouse, American Tobacco, Heinz, Lorillard, and Union Carbide.[26] In 1941 the *Post* was described by the historian, Arthur M. Schlesinger, as " . . . the dinosaur among the periodicals."[27] The magazine was seen and read everywhere and people knew it as they knew their own names.

Advertising Research

Before 1920 advertisers and their agencies, for the most part, accepted the efficacy of advertising largely on faith. John Caples, one of the early advertising researchers as a vice-president of Batten, Barton, Durstine & Osborn, attested to the fact that there was very little evidence of the effect of advertising on magazine readers. Many companies believed that, if other corporations which had been advertising in magazines were successful, then advertising in itself must be productive.[28] Later on, market research became an important basis of product improvement, and national advertising became important as a means of capitalizing on product improvement.

Advertising men turned to research to document the effectiveness of magazine advertising and one of the leaders in market research, which became an important part of national magazine advertising, was the Curtis Publishing Company.[29]

George Horace Lorimer

In 1934 George Horace Lorimer, considered to be a conservative and common-sense businessman, as well as a great editor, moved up from the presidency to the board chairmanship of the Curtis Publishing Company with almost absolute control. In Fred Healey he had a strong advertising director to help him.[30] It was said that, at this time, the dean of Wharton School of Business of the University of Pennsylvania advised a Curtis Publishing Company executive, who happened to be his friend, to leave the company. The academician stated that Lorimer was no businessman and would wreck the company.[31]

Curtis Publishing Company was strong at this time, but competition was mounting. *Collier's* was inferior to the *Post* according to experts, and *Liberty Magazine* was considered by Lorimer to be cheap. *Time* had moved up as a competitor, and in 1936 both *Life* and *Look* were founded. These were picture magazines. The Curtis magazines, particularly the *Post*, were still dominant in circulation and as advertising media.[32]

When Lorimer moved up to board chairman of Curtis, there were strong contenders for the company's presidency. The most competent was advertising director Healey. He was a power in the company, eminently qualified, and he wanted the job. However, he did not get it. Instead, the company chose Walter D. Fuller to be president at the end of 1934. Fuller had sold subscriptions for the *Ladies' Home Journal* as a boy, worked as a bank clerk, and had become office manager for the Crowell Publishing Company.[33]

AFTER WORLD WAR II

Magazine advertising continued to be successful after World War II. In the early twenties a magazine publisher considered himself successful if his magazine grossed $2 million a year in such revenue. After the war some magazines carried that much advertising in a single issue.[34] The *Ladies' Home Journal* issue of October 1946 contained 246 pages, and its advertising revenue from 334 advertisers amounted to $2,146,746. In 1947, the fiftieth anniversary of the Curtis Publishing Company management of the *Post*, advertising revenue totaled $59,529,458.[35]

Auditing Circulation

The Association of American Advertisers made the first attempt, in 1899, to verify circulations of magazines on a uniform standard basis. The Audit Bureau of Circulations (ABC) was founded in 1914. At first, it was difficult to induce publishers to join the association. Even Cyrus Curtis hesitated joining and stated: "No one doubts the circulation statements of my company."[36] However, the list of ABC magazine publications, including the *Post*, lengthened over the years, and by 1944 there were 212 members.[37]

Important Research Study

For many years, the *Post* claimed that its biggest dimension was its readers' belief in and respect and affection for the magazine. It had relied largely on its audited circulation and its claim that people believed advertising more when they read it in the *Post*, while other publications were making promotional capital out of audience studies. In October 1949, it announced a huge and imposing piece of research to back up its contentions.

This survey investigated 30,800 households. The researchers also queried readers of two other weeklies, *Life* and *Collier's*, and one biweekly, *Look*. The research, which was designed and conducted by the Curtis Publishing Company's National Analysts, Inc., Philadelphia, under researcher Arnold King, combined two separate studies into one.[38]

Of major importance was the analysis of the findings concerning the differences between the *Post* readers and those of the other three publications. The object of the exercise was to measure the *Post's* impact on individuals by asking carefully defined readers a set of specific questions.

A reader was defined as one who 1) could produce for inspection at least one of the last four issues of any of the four magazines included; and 2) stated that he or she read regularly at least two out of every four issues. Readers were also asked how much time they usually spent on each magazine; how many times they "picked it up" on the average, that is, how often they went back to continue reading it; in which magazine they paid most attention to the advertising; and in which one they had the most confidence in the products advertised.[39]

Some of the findings of this study were: 1) the *Post* found it had an average reading time of close to three hours for each reader; 2) *Collier's* had slightly more than 2-1/2 hours; and 3) *Life* and *Look* each had 1 hour and 35 minutes.[40]

On the average number of times readers picked up the magazines, the *Post* was ahead with 4.91 times; *Collier's* next with 4.36; *Look* third with 3.43; and *Life* fourth with 3.22 times.[41]

What was more interesting from a promotional standpoint for the *Post* were the statistics on the last two words of its slogan "big-believed-beloved." Reporting these results in a series of "duplicated" readers, the study compared separately the impact of the *Post* and one or more of the other magazines. Of those surveyed 58.9 percent said they believed the *Post* more reliable; among the readers of *Life* and one or more of the publications, 51.1 percent thought *Life* more reliable. Among those found to qualify as both the *Post* and *Life* readers, 65 percent said the *Post* was more reliable; 35 percent *Life*; 13.2 percent *Collier's*; and 9.8 percent *Look*.[42]

In addition to the findings mentioned above, there were some highly reassuring figures for the Curtis Publishing Company on the quality of the *Post* family. For example, data were uncovered showing that 53 percent of the *Post*'s households enjoyed an annual income of $4,000 or over; 70.5 percent owned their own homes; 79 percent possessed automobiles; and 83 percent mechanical refrigeration.[43]

At the time the above study was announced, the Curtis Publishing Company published other equally optimistic statistics. They reported that advertising and circulation revenues had both increased for the first half of 1949. Curtis realized a profit of $3,245,679 on $71,610,652 worth of business.[44]

New Developments

The *Post*, which was the giant of the magazine world in 1947, had the audacity to announce that they would soon not only raise their newsstand price and subscription price, but that they would also raise their advertising rates. Beginning with the issue dated November 15, 1947, the newsstand price of the *Post* went from 10 to 15 cents, and the annual subscription went from $5 to $6.[45]

Advertising rates were raised an average of 6.6 percent effective with the issue of April 3, 1948. The black and white page rate prior to the increase was $10,500.[46]

The *Post* had done away with its original nickel-a-copy price in April 1942. The Crowell-Collier Publishing Company quickly followed this precedent with an increase to 10 cents a copy for *Collier's*.[47]

The *Post* claimed that the reason for its decisions was the cost pinch they were suffering. The average price of magazine paper was around $182 a ton compared with $150 a year earlier. As Walter D. Fuller, president of Curtis, stated:

> The rapidly increasing cost of materials, transportation and other items over which we have little control, is very disturbing to the management, principally because there seems to be no stopping the trend in this direction. It is very difficult to keep prices of our products and services in line with costs.[48]

Fuller considered himself a cost-cutting curator for the Curtis board of directors and the Curtis trustees. He viewed the Curtis Publishing Company as big business, and he realized that to be a successful magazine publisher he must be sensitive to changing public taste and that his response must often come as much from quickness of wit as from cost analysis. Under Fuller, the Curtis Publishing Company became a completely integrated magazine-publishing enterprise.[49]

Fuller was known to have mingled with the heads of other corporations in meetings of the American Manufacturers Association of which he became president at one time. He remained as president of the Curtis Publishing Company until 1950, and then continued as the chief executive of the company until 1957, when he stepped down as chairman. He remained a member of the board and served on one of its executive committees. He spent 56 years with the Curtis Publishing Company.[50]

One of the important developments under Fuller was a subsidiary known as the Curtis Circulation Company. It had branch offices in principal cities throughout the United States. It distributed all Curtis magazines to over 100,000 newsstand dealers. Benjamin Allen was the head of the Circulation Company, and he was largely responsible for its continued success.[51]

A New Editor

When Lorimer resigned in 1937, Wesley W. Stout became the editor of the *Post*, but did not last long. According to some historians, Stout lacked the judgment and tact of Lorimer, and he was under pressure to keep costs down. Among other problems, he had the misfortune to run into World War II. It drew people's attention to more immediate matters and left advertisers with nothing to advertise except their names, and the supply of magazine paper was drastically cut. Stout was also victimized by his own mistaken judgment. He ran several stories on the Jews: the first was "Red-White-and-Blue Herring," by Jerome Frank; the second "Jews are Different," by Waldo Frank. These two stories were not protested. However, on March 28, 1942, he published "The Case against the Jews," by Martin Mayer, and there was an explosion. Cries of anti-Semitism were raised, subscriptions were cancelled, some advertising schedules were jerked out of the magazine, copies of the *Post* were torn from newsstand counters and destroyed, and the damage was done. The *Post* was already in trouble and Stout, in disfavor, had no choice but to resign.[52]

Ben Hibbs

Ben Hibbs, then just past 40, succeeded Stout as editor in 1942. He had taught journalism for two years at Kansas State College. In 1940 he became editor of *Country Gentleman*, and took over the editorship of the *Post* at a time as trying and tremulous as any in the long history of the magazine. The two surest statistical barometers of magazine success, circulation and advertising revenue, indicated an unsettled condition. Circulation under Stout moved upward from 3,003,015 copies in 1937 to a net paid total of 3,385,738 for 1941.[53] But there was real concern over whether circulation and advertising would hold up during a global war in which the United States suddenly found itself engaged.[54]

Editor Hibbs' first declaration of policy was simple and to the point.

> I think the processes of Democracy should not be suspended during the war. I believe that constructive criticism during wartime is not only patriotic but urgently necessary. The problems that confront the American people are staggering. It is our responsibility to weigh, analyze and explain these problems. America's life will be affected by what happens in Brazil—in Turkey—in Hong Kong—in Russia. To the greatest degree in its History the *Post* will report and interpret these happenings.[55]

Curtis Publishing Company had other problems such as the lack of foresight on the part of the trustees of the company when they passed up an opportunity to diversify in 1941. At that time the National Broadcasting Company operated both a Red and Blue Network. However, the Federal Communications Commission forced it to divest itself of part of its operation, and it offered the Blue

Network to the Curtis Publishing Company. Curtis refused the network, and it later became the American Broadcasting Company. In later years Curtis had the opportunity to purchase the Columbia Broadcasting System for about $10 million. It also declined this offer. It did not so much resist change as ignore it. It had what one editor later described as a "toplofty attitude." [56] The *Post* improved in many ways under Hibbs' editorship, and in four years was back on its feet and steadily improving. Circulation, at nearly 3.5 million in 1942, went to 4 million in 1947. The magazine stood first among general weekly magazines in number of advertising pages with gross revenue of $24,368,000 for the first six months of 1946. [57] On May 22, 1942, J. Frank Seaman, the promotion manager, sent a letter to newspaper editors throughout the country enclosing a copy of the issue for May 30. He labeled it a "precedent-smashing issue" and gave editors permission to quote up to 500 words from an article entitled "This War Will Save Private Enterprise," by Thurmond Arnold.*

From 1942 on, Hibbs proceeded to prove that high editorial standards would attract readers and advertisers. An important innovation was a completely new format for the magazine. So drastic was the change in appearance that some of the old compositors considered it verged on sacrilege. Most of the changes were made within one month, although the refining process continued for six months. When Hibbs became editor, the editorial staff as listed on the masthead consisted of 11 people. Within a few years that list quintupled. The editorial expansion led to a departure from the long-time policy of one-man editorship. Although Hibbs continued to be the final arbiter, he delegated authority to associates including the executive editor, the managing editor, and the art editor. The *Post*'s covers continued to be famous, and their war correspondents began to file dispatches that increased the volume of firsthand war observations and greatly enhanced the vitality of the magazine. Norman Rockwell was the notable cover artist. Some of the outstanding stories were written by Joseph E. Davies, Cecil S. Forester, Captain Harry C. Butcher, and General Holland M. Smith. During this time Hibbs and the magazine were awarded many honors. [58]

The May 3, 1953 issue even carried a full page editorial. The *Post* rarely endorsed a presidential condidate prior to nomination, but it went all out in its urging of the nomination of general of the Army Dwight D. Eisenhower as Republican candidate for president. [59]

---

*See Appendix C.

A record high in *Post* sales was established with the February 14, 1953 issue which featured the first of ten installments on the life of Bing Crosby, entitled "Call Me Lucky." Sales for that issue reached 4,935,000 copies, an increase of 464,000 over the previous week. The *Post's* circulation hit a new high of 5 million during an eight-part series by Arthur Godfrey, entitled "This is My Story," which began November 5, 1955.[60]

Robert E. MacNeal

Fuller resigned from the chairmanship of the Curtis Publishing Company in 1957, although he continued as a director. Robert E. MacNeal, who had succeeded Fuller as president of Curtis in 1950, became chief executive officer in 1955. MacNeal took that office after 32 years with the company. Starting in 1923, he became assistant secretary in 1937, a director in 1942, secretary in 1943, and vice-president in 1949.[61]

Healey, who was advertising director of the Curtis Publishing Company which, of course, included the *Post*, continued in that position until his death in 1947 following a heart attack. He was succeeded by Arthur Kohler. Kohler's first major problem was the *Post* which, at that time, was second to *Life* magazine in circulation. This was upsetting to the whole Curtis Company, particularly to the advertising representatives of the *Post* who were attempting to convince advertisers that circulation was not that important.[62]

Circulation and Audience Studies

Ever since 1941, the year the Audit Bureau of Circulations was founded, when selling advertising space, magazines had been content to rely on certified circulation figures provided by the bureau. As radio's vast audiences were reported, circulation figures in magazines seemed woefully small. *Life* magazine adopted the idea of total readership of a magazine. This idea was presented to them by Alfred M. Politz who not only sold it to *Life* but was also quite successful in selling it to several other magazines.

The total audience figure included not only the original subscriber or newsstand buyer, but also pass-along readers in the purchaser's household or outside of it. Therefore, one single copy of a magazine might be read by four, five, six, or even more people. *Look* magazine liked the idea and it, too, came up with a huge total audience figure. Curtis rejected the technique and continued to use ABC figures.

The *Post*'s research department conducted studies to show that people paid more attention to advertising in its pages because they believed in the editorial quality of the magazine. Later, they embarked upon a research technique called "Issue Exposure Days," and in 1958 a thick report was titled "Ad Page Exposure." It indicated how often a page of advertising was exposed to readers and what the readers were like. The *Post*'s salesmen did not receive this enthusiastically. They indicated that they wished the money had been spent in buying circulation that would have put the *Post* ahead of *Life*. Next, Curtis published a new giant Politz study underwritten jointly by the *Post* and the *Reader's Digest*.

The findings of this study were presented to an audience of agency and advertising men at the Waldorf-Astoria Hotel on January 22, 1960. Personal interviews had been conducted with 32,000 respondents in a national probability sample. Although there was initial enthusiasm shown by Curtis executives and *Post* salesmen, the research was considered by the advertising community as an extravagant exercise in statistical virtuosity on themes which few understood and almost nobody could put to practical use.

The *Post* was losing business; the number of advertising pages fell from 3,687 in 1954 to 2,816 in 1959.[63] The company's attempts to rectify the situation took several directions, none of which proved fruitful. The nature of the business seemed to have changed beyond the power of management to grasp it. Editor Hibbs, for example, complained: "What in heaven's name has happened to the publishing business that it has become so incredibly more complex than it was forty or fifty years ago?"[64]

Hibbs found it so complex that he resigned on January 6, 1962, after a 20-year tenure, and deferred to a younger man, Robert Fuoss, who stepped aside two months later, to be succeeded by Robert Lee Sherrod. On April 1, 1962, Curtis announced sweeping format changes of the *Post*, and some editorial and business staff operational revisions. In making his announcement MacNeal, the 58-year-old president said, "The rapid acceleration of social, economic and technological developments of recent years has made it clear that magazines no longer can operate under the concept of business as usual."[65]

TROUBLE AHEAD

Rumor clouds began gathering darkly over the Curtis Publishing Company's sedate white stone headquarters on Philadelphia's historic Independence Square during the fall of 1961. The venerable firm tried to give them a silver lining in a series of exuberant full-page newspaper advertisements calling attention to the revamped *Post* ("Suddenly Reading Becomes an Adventure") and the *Ladies' Home Journal* ("When the Journal Speaks, Women Listen").[66]

Plainly, Curtis was in trouble, and its cause was not helped by persistent reports that corporate raiders, anxious to purchase the company for a quick killing, were quietly buying stock. "These stories are vicious,"[67] angrily snapped MacNeal, ordinarily a mild-mannered man. "I'm not going to say anything because there isn't anything to say. When there is, I'll say it. Believe me."[68]

March 1962 appeared to signal the start of rapid decline. Operating losses were $11.2 million at the close of 1961. It was also the twelfth year of steady decline for the *Post* with a loss of 20.4 percent in advertising pages. Its gross advertising revenue had fallen almost $18 million in 1961, from $103,930,304 to $86,442,603.[69]

Mathew J. Culligan

The Curtis board of directors decided on a drastic move. After a long search on the outside, they decided to accept the resignation of MacNeal, who had been president for 14 years, and on July 9, 1962, appointed Mathew J. Culligan, formerly of the Interpublic Advertising Agency and the National Broadcasting Company as president.[70]

Culligan's record of his first meeting with the board is interesting:

> I stepped into the cavernous, dimly lit, paneled boardroom. The twelve directors stood. Each extended his hand as I moved around the table. As I shook each hand, its owner said, "Welcome, Mr. President."
>
> Albert Linton bade me sit at his right. I did. He continued as chairman of the meeting as I sat quietly at his side, studying the directors, most of whom I was seeing for the first time. Linton's long description of my background gave me time to settle down and look around. First I glanced at Bob MacNeal, who seemed to have shrunk since our previous meeting. He huddled in the massive boardroom chair, saying not a word and looking dreadfully ill. I studied each director carefully and tried to imagine what lay behind his appearance.[71]

He was hired at a salary of $130,000 a year, with a five-year contract. He brought with him a whole new crew of executives, mostly from the National Broadcasting Company or other magazines. He also distributed vice-presidencies with various titles, and even appointed a new editorial director, Clay Blair, Jr., and designated him a vice-president.[72]

Culligan decimated department after department—retired some executives and fired others. Following this internal disruption, he went off on a barnstorming trip visiting 100 top advertisers and the 30 leading advertising agencies, promising new life, new blood, dynamic marketing, and new purpose for the corporation. He claimed that in his first 32 months as chief executive he was responsible for the sale of $78 million in advertising and brought about a cost saving of $13 million annually.[73] Despite these heroics, Curtis lost $18,917,000 in 1962.[74]

Culligan brought in John MacLain Clifford in October 1962 as executive vice-president for finance and operations. Clifford immediately moved in on a cost reduction program of a 20 percent cut across the board.[75]

Following Culligan's first 18-month period as president, the following appeared in *Newsweek*:

As head of one of the oldest publishing companies in America, Culligan has slashed annual expenses by $16 million, trimmed 2,300 employees off the payroll, pared company losses from $18.9 million in 1962 to $3.4 million in 1963, and brought the *Saturday Evening Post* flagship of the five-magazine Curtis fleet, its first profitable quarter in two years. Yet Curtis, owing $22 million in short-term debt due last summer, was still in trouble. Hampered further by libel suits against the *Post* (now totaling about $25 million, including a record $3,060,000 award to former Georgia football coach Wally Butts), and almost crippled by Madison Avenue rumors Curtis was going under, supersalesman Culligan sold himself and the company's future to a superfinancier, Serge Semenenko of the First National Bank of Boston. "Curtis is a wonderful name in publishing, and we decided in Boston not to have it go into the ashcan." said Semenenko. "I had faith in Joe Culligan and I promised I would get him the money he needed to carry on."[76]

Semenenko kept his word allowing Curtis to convert its $22 million in short-term debt into long term (five years) loans, extend the maturity of an $8.5 million debt owed by its subsidiary paper company, and still have $4.5 million for working capital.[77]

The advertising news was encouraging. C. L. MacNelly, newly appointed publisher of the *Post*, stated in Detroit, where he was soliciting automotive advertising, "Television is leveling off; two years from now the magazines that still are in business will be in a position to benefit."[78] That statement was about as inaccurate as some of the others made by *Post* executives during these difficult times.

As usual, in trying corporate situations, the publisher was changing almost yearly. Marvin D. Kantor, chairman of the Curtis Magazine Division, appointed Jess L. Ballew, vice-president of the Curtis Publishing Company, to publisher of the *Post* on August 31, 1964. Ballew had first joined the *Post* in 1954, and at the time of his appointment was advertising director.[79]

Damaging Libel Suits

Two football coaches, Wallace Butts, University of Georgia, and Paul Bryant, University of Alabama, individually brought libel suits against the *Post* for a total of $10 million. These suits were the result of a story published on March 23, 1963, "The Story of a Football Fix." On September 19, 1964, the ex-president of the Chrysler Corporation sued for $2 million. Libel suits are routine in the magazine publishing business, but the *Post* was setting new records. Although some suits were dropped, and others settled out of court, libel suits against Curtis reached a reported $40 million. This amount of money exceeded the $35 million loan obtained in November 1963, from a syndicate of five banks spearheaded by Semenenko.[80]

Nevertheless, it had begun to look as though the salesmanship and wholesale firings by Culligan might pay off. The Curtis loss in 1963 was only $4,393,000. This was a big improvement over the year before, and great things were prophesied for 1964.[81]

The Start of the Curtis Revolt

Early in 1964, Culligan learned of a proposal by Marvin Kantor, a senior vice-president, and Clay Blair, Jr., senior vice-president and editor of the *Post*, that had been sent to the board of directors at the May board meeting. The intent was to induce a majority of the board to vote Marvin Kantor into the presidency and to make Culligan chairman of the board. The first move of these two senior vice-presidents was to approach Semenenko and attempt to clear their strategy with him. He replied that the banks would not accept any change in the management of Curtis. Culligan assumed that their ploy having failed, Blair and Kantor would resign. They did not and, as Culligan found out later, actually began to plan a major "Palace Rebellion" in the summer of 1964.[82] Culligan contemplated dismissing Blair and Kantor, then thought better of it. He wrote that Blair was turning out a good and, at times, a very good *Post*. Blair and

Kantor led a group of 17 editorial and executive dissidents in this uprising. Their ultimatum to Culligan was that unless he resigned, none of them would report for work on the following Monday, and there would be no *Post* three weeks hence. Months of friction, infighting, and cut-throat conflict had preceded this ultimatum.[83] Then, on September 29, 1964, a letter was addressed to M. Albert Linton, chairman of the executive committee of the Curtis Publishing Company, outlining the basis of the revolt, and castigating Culligan, in detail, requesting that he be stripped of his executive power. The letter was signed by 15 Curtis executives.[84]

Culligan's Problems

It was evident that the worst problem at Curtis in the early 1960s was not advertising sales or editorial quality, but the banks. Soon after Culligan had taken over as president, the banks asked him how he proposed to repay them the $22 million that was due on August 16, 1962.[85] Although the principal bank, First National City of New York, made it clear they were unhappy, Culligan, with his customary enthusiasm, talked the banks into a year's extension and even into increasing the loan by $4 million. As the year 1964 began, it appeared that the salvation of Curtis was almost in sight. The corporate losses had been cut by almost 80 percent. A long-term $35 million bank loan had been approved, and the new management faced the future with high hopes.[86]

It was not long before a conflict between Blair, the editorial director, and Clifford developed.

> The conflict between Clifford and Blair came quickly and inevitably. They fought over every one of the technical and financial problems that lie at the heart of corporate power. "During 1963, Clifford got a throttle hold on the company." Blair said later. "He took over circulation, manufacturing, and paper mills, then accounting, personnel, and legal. He brought in three obnoxious lieutenants: Maurice Poppei, controller; Gloria Swett, legal; Sidney Natkin, personnel. By summer, Clifford's control of money and people was so complete that noboby, including me, could hire or fire or give a raise or sign a check without his specific approval."[87]

Culligan received a temporary reprieve from the Blair onslaught in April 1964. It was announced that Texas Gulf Sulphur had discovered major deposits of copper, zinc, and silver, valued at up to $2 billion, just 300 feet from 110,000 acres owned by the T. S. Woollings Company, a Canadian subsidiary of Curtis. Immediately Curtis stock rose from $6 to $19.25 a share.[88]

Blair and Kantor finally decided on a courageous confrontation with Culligan at the October 1, 1964 Curtis executive committee meeting, just before the next day's board meeting. They accused Culligan of malicious management and offered their resignations which were refused. Culligan fought back and the settlement of the issue was postponed until the next day's board meeting. The story leaked out in the *Gallagher Report* and the *New York Times*. Headlines such as, "Curtis Editors Accuse Chief of Mismanagement," and "Curtis Aids Vow to Press Growth," did not help the *Post* or the other Curtis magazines.[89]

Finally, Blair and Kantor's uprising backfired, and on October 11, 1964, the board fired both of them. The headlines in the *New York Times* read as follows:

Curtis Suspends Two Culligan Critics
Blair and Kantor Relieved of Duties in Policy Rift[90]

Blair, whose salary was $75,000 a year and Kantor, who was being paid $80,000 a year, filed suits against Curtis, claiming they had been wrongfully discharged and demanded $36,250 as accrued compensation, and unearned sums for the balance of their contracts totaling $500,000. In a settlement, made on December 24, 1964, each man accepted $75,000.[91]

An Attempt as a Biweekly

In November 1964, the management of the *Post* decided to convert it into a biweekly in a cost-cutting attempt to save its life. Taking a page from the television industry's promotional efforts, magazine publishers began developing the total audience concept of magazine readership.[92] To determine what magazines labeled "pass along" readership, research organizations began counting people who thumbed through someone else's copy of a magazine, as well as the person who subscribed to it or bought it at a newsstand.

During this period the *Post* boosted its advertising rates and this cost it much linage. In 1953 it had 1,042 advertisers. In 1963 it had only 468. Curtis also drastically liberalized discounts from basic page rates in force in 1962. By July 1964, advertisers earning one or more of these discounts accounted for half of the *Post*'s advertising volume.[93]

Culligan's Downfall

Culligan wrote a full rebuttal to the September 29, 1964 letter which had been sent to the Curtis board and signed by 15 executives demanding Culligan's removal. This rebuttal was delivered on October 9, 1964. An investigative committee was appointed to make its report at a board meeting scheduled for October 19, 1964.[94] The committee called in all the signatories of the letter and questioned them as to their knowledge of the charges. An official letter, dated October 19, 1964, was later sent to Culligan, closing out the investigation.[95]

At the October 19, 1964 board meeting, Culligan resigned as president of Curtis and remained as chairman of the board. The board offered the job to several men including Edward Miller, publisher of *McCall's*, and Raymond MacGranahan, of the Times-Mirror Company. Both turned it down. Finally they promoted Clifford from executive vice-president to the presidency. Over the next few weeks, Culligan claimed there were various harassments, and it was obvious that Clifford did not want him in office. Culligan resigned as chairman on January 17, 1965.[96] He had lasted just over two years as head of the company. He had been in charge during the period when the company lost nearly $19 million in 1962, over $4 million in 1963, and $13.9 million in 1964. Under the terms of his contract he received $110,000 in 1966, and for ten years thereafter received $20,093 annually.[97]

Martin Ackerman

During the second week of April 1968, it was evident to all concerned that something drastic had to be done to save the company. The First National Bank of Boston, which was owed $9 million, met with Martin Ackerman, 36 years old, and president of Perfect Film Corporation. The bank was impressed with his background and recommended him to the Curtis board. On April 22, 1968, he was named to the Curtis presidency without salary by the board. He had $5 million to invest in the company, and he was the only one who would take the position.[98]

At Ackerman's first meeting with Curtis employees he intoned, "My name is Marty Ackerman, I am very rich, and I intend to make all of you very rich too."[99] He decided that, in order to convert a magazine that was losing money, he had three possible options: cut costs, induce subscribers to pay more for the magazine, or sell more advertising.[100]

On May 11, 1968, Ackerman announced some changes in the operation of the *Post*, which had become Curtis's most troubled property. His plan called for reducing the physical size of the magazine and redirecting its editorial product to appeal to high-income, suburban, and big city readers.[101] To accomplish this, he made a deal which was announced jointly by him and James A. Linen, president of Time Inc.

> Time will advance Curtis $5,000,000 in badly needed working capital for an "indefinite" period.
> Time Inc.'s *Life* magazine signed a printing contract with Curtis that runs until June 30, 1970. Curtis's wholly owned Sharon Hill printing plant has been heavily dependent on the *Post* to keep its presses running. The *Life* contract will fill some of the holes left by the *Post*'s truncated circulation.
> Time Inc. will throw its magazine distribution and subscription sales business to Curtis's profitable circulation subsidiaries. This will sweeten another deal in which Curtis will sell off its circulation operations to Ackerman's Perfect Film on terms not yet decided.
> In return for all this, *Life*, whose advertising sales have been lagging, gets an inexpensive way to pull ahead of *Look* in circulation.[102]

The benefits for the *Post* were threefold: 1) its reduced but upgraded circulation made it a more selective advertising medium; 2) it was more attractive to advertisers because its advertising rates dropped from $27,585 for each black and white page to $12,780, in line with its reduced circulation; and 3) advertising agency executives voiced the opinion that the *Post* in its new incarnation would be living in a different competitive environment.[103]

As a result of this move, *Life*'s circulation increased by nearly 500,000 new subscribers, which, added to its 7.6 million circulation, put it ahead of *Look*'s 7.8 million.[104]

Ackerman described Time Inc.'s $5 million advance as an "indefinite" loan. He said that, although final terms had not been worked out, Time Inc. would provide $2.5 million in July and $2.5 million in September 1968. Repayment would be made in offering the use of printing facilities and subscription services.[105]

On June 15, 1968, to dramatize these precedent-setting moves, the *Post* published a graphically changed "A" edition distributed among 20,000 agency and advertiser executives. This special edition, which could well be considered the forerunner of present-day demographic editions such as *Time*'s "*Time B*" and *Newsweek*'s "*Executive Newsweek*" editions, contained an editorial written by Ackerman.

> Authorities in the magazine field will testify that this is an unprecedented step—for a large publication to eschew hypocrisy of

forced circulation, the debasing appeals to a lowest common denominator. It is unheard of for a magazine to release uncongenial readers in order that it may better serve the most vital portion of its readership.[106]

Ackerman appointed Stephen E. Kelly vice-president and publisher of the *Post* in May 1968, and on July 26, 1968, Kelly sent out a letter to advertisers and agencies describing an advertising rate protective plan.[107]

THE BEGINNING OF THE END

A plan was announced in August 1968 whereby the advertising sales staffs of *Holiday* and the *Post* would be consolidated in a cost-cutting move. Each salesperson on both staffs would be assigned a quota of advertising pages and would receive a bonus for exceeding it, over and above his/her base salary.[108]

Not long after he took office, Ackerman met with editor William Emerson and managing editor Otto Friedrich, and made the following statement:

We've got to have more editorial excitement, all through the *Post*, on every page . . .

. . . let me make one thing clear: I intend to participate in the editorial direction of the *Post*, okay?

. . . I've put my five million dollars on the line. I've staked my reputation, my career, and my money on the proposition that I can get Curtis to make a profit. Now if I make that kind of a commitment, I'm going to *participate* in the editorial direction of these magazines, okay? Because if I can't participate, then I'm not interested in putting up my five million dollars, okay? So what I mean is, I don't want to edit the magazine, but I want the magazine to reflect me. I want it to reflect my personality.[109]

Ackerman attempted to play editor of the *Post* for a short period of time, but soon found himself embroiled in business management problems. The deal with Time Inc. caused management problems involving circulation subscription contracts. The halving of the *Post*'s circulation threatened every other part of the corporation. The paper plant would, in the future, be asked for only half as much paper, and the giant printing presses would stand idle for hours every week.[110]

The day after the announcement of the deal with Time Inc., Ackerman publicly acknowledged that Curtis had suffered a "large loss" in the first quarter of 1968 and would lose a great deal more during the rest of the year.[111] Since Curtis stock had been removed from the New York Stock Exchange, there was no need of an exact quarterly statement of profit or loss.

As in all commercial magazines, the *Post* was dependent upon advertising revenue for survival. Chris Welles commented: "The problem with the *Post*, which suffered 18 successive years of advertising decline, was that, in never adjusting to the age of television, it had the distinct, unavoidable smell of a loser."[112]

During this period, Robert Engelke, media director of Wells, Rich, Greene Advertising Agency, may have summed up the impressions of a majority of the advertising buyers of the country when he said:

> The internal political situation of a medium, or whether it is losing money or not, is not really any of our business. It ought to be that we are buying so much circulation at such a price. But unfortunately, we all tend to make it our business. You have to understand this is a very frightened industry. Our livelihood is at the whim of our clients, and we'll go a long way to avoid being criticized. Now there's nothing really wrong with advertising in the last issue of a magazine. But if we were to recommend a medium, and it folded a half-dozen issues later, it might mean we were out of touch, that our judgment was wrong. Everybody likes to stick with a winner.
>
> We might have been able to help if we had had some real assurance that the *Post* was planning to stay in business. When Ackerman came in, everyone knew his background and was suspicious. We wondered: Was he sincere or was it all to be some tax dodge? Was it really too late to do anything? Could Ackerman do anything even if it wasn't too late? So we held off. Numbers didn't have that much to do with it—the *Post*'s numbers are not a long way from *Life*'s or *Look*'s, but if you can have *Life* or *Look*, why take a chance with the *Post*? I suppose it was just this sort of thing that drove them further to the wall. But we weren't being malicious. We all hate to see any medium closed on us. It was just good business thinking.[113]

Ackerman's enthusiasm and optimism changed in December 1969, when he discovered that publisher Kelly's advertising page projections for the *Post* were a "lot of blue sky." While Kelly was projecting 1,000 pages of advertising, up from 1968's 904 pages which would have turned a $1 million profit, Ackerman's private auditing firm showed only 850 to 900 pages, and a corresponding loss of from $1.9 million to $3.5 million. The *Post* lost $3.5 million in 1967.[114]

AFTER 148 YEARS OF PUBLISHING—THE END

At the start of 1969 it became evident to Ackerman and the directors of the Curtis Publishing Company that there was no way the *Post* could be pulled out of its financial difficulties. On January 10, 1969, Ackerman called a news conference and announced that the February 8, 1969 issue of the *Post* would be the magazine's last.[115]

At the news conference Ackerman stated that the *Post* had operated in 1968 at a loss of about $5 million. He told how he had raised $15 million in new capital, but that continued publication of the magazine would have resulted in a $3 million loss in 1969. He summarized his feelings in a closing statement, "Apparently there is just not the need for our product in today's scheme of living."[116]

On January 10, 1969, Ackerman also addressed a letter to the employees attempting to explain the recent turn of events.*

THE AFTERMATH

The sounding of the death knell at the *Post* was followed by the resignations of two directors of the Curtis Publishing Company, Robert D. Hedberg and Alfred E. Driscoll. Driscoll, a former governor of New Jersey, said he had joined the board in 1967 because of his affection for the now defunct magazine. "My hope was that something could be done to save it. When that failed my mission was lost."[117]

Ackerman was asked to resign by the Curtis board of directors, and he did so at the March 1969 board meeting. He was replaced by G. B. McCombs, who had recently been promoted to senior vice-president, after being with Curtis since 1930.[118]

McCombs lasted five weeks as president, and the position then went to Philip Kalodner, a young Philadelphia lawyer and representative of minority stockholders. The board of directors of Curtis, depleted by the resignations of Ackerman, Milton Gould, and McCombs, now consisted of only six members (one of whom was serving as U.S. Ambassador to Saigon).[119]

Writing in *Advertising Age* on February 10, 1969, Herbert D. Maneloveg, vice-president and media director of Batten, Barton,

---

*See copy of letter in Appendix E.

Durstine & Osborne, outlined why the *Post* was a lesson in how not to market a magazine:

> All of us (infused with a tone of self-ordained authority) can point out reasons for the *Post's* demise. Singularly and collectively, each excuse makes eminent sense. But the death of a once proud publishing venture is, in reality, an accumulation of a hundred sins of omission and commission, lost opportunities, financially foolhardy blunders, and misspent directions too numerous to recount.
>
> It doesn't ever happen overnight. It takes decades to destroy a solid force such as Curtis' flagship. And, ironically, through it all, the publication held on longer than the doom merchants and vulturistic competitors thought possible. Yet it could have survived, and should have.
>
> My basic point! It was not the *product* that was bad (this is what most readers of the statement will think), but rather the manufacturer of that product who for many, many years didn't truly understand "today's scheme of living" or today's scheme of marketing, to put it another way. That's the phrase in the sentence that counts.
>
> For some totally unfathomable reason, a large number of magazine publishers fail to examine their handiwork as if it were a product, not unlike an item advertised in the magazine itself. The publication should be studied as an entity that calls for proper distribution, timely promotion, correct pricing, dynamic packaging, and adequate consumer awareness through advertising, as well as sound salesmanship to propel it forward. And all these elements must be balanced together in the proper proportions.
>
> Too often, these magazine manufacturers concentrate only on the editorial product. They forget about the other market. They somehow expect the consumer (the advertiser) to gobble it up without the manufacturer adroitly folding the critical and salient marketing factors into the mix. It's this nonmarketing approach that helped ruin the *Post*.
>
> "Today's scheme of living" demands of the manufacturer that his customer be convinced that the product is right. The brand, whether it be an automobile or a magazine, can't do it by itself. There are many, many good products that flounder because of inadequate marketing direction, and that's what occurred at the *Post*. It's a lesson that should be emblazoned on the minds of all publishers, and remembered forever.
>
> Need a few examples? Take distribution. The *Post* certainly had enough circulation, yet it always seemed to be in the wrong place. For the past 20 years, America's advertisers called for coverage in the major cities because that's where the population was moving. Many magazines were cognizant of this and followed

accordingly. But the *Post* kept building it elsewhere. The circulation people justified their position by saying it was profitable circulation. But was it if the advertiser didn't respond? It's bottom line profit that counts with a company, not certain individual departments. "Blinder marketing" is what occurred here.

... Magazines have historically priced themselves in a most peculiar manner, one in which poor advertising publications inevitably get poorer. These people usually offered such price cutting deals that it took years of renewals to eventually get the money back. In most businesses, home delivery is obviously more expensive than when a person shops for the product on the stands; magazines followed the opposite strategy. When they learned their lesson and started to adjust the price of subscriptions, it was too late. For the *Post*, and for others as well.

... Granted there were negatives working against the *Post*, such as demographics and pass-along audience, but there are drawbacks inherent in every medium. The magazine developed no consistent theme, no steady advertising thrust, no advertising-oriented research, little sales-gaited promotion.

It wandered, for decades, all over the lot. In an age when total audience came to the fore, the *Post* failed to concentrate with sufficient enthusiasm on the pluses that could sometimes override a potential numerical advantage offered up by a competitor. One sales administration after another floundered. None gave its salesmen a viable idea to work against. It was almost as if each salesman were on his own. Two more marketing tools went unharnessed.

Yes, the product could have been right, perhaps imperfect, but not that much different from a lot of other products. After all, it did satisfy millions of readers. But the people who produced the product forgot about "today's scheme of marketing," and specifically forgot that they had two distinct marketing problems. The *Post* struggled through, concentrating on one—editorial—fumbling on the other. And that spelled disaster. A disaster that never should have happened.[120]

The Coming of Beurt R. SerVaas

In May 1970, the trustees sold 700,000 shares of Curtis stock they had controlled to Beurt R. SerVaas, a self-made millionaire from Indianapolis, Indiana, who took over control as president and principal stockholder. He related his initial actions as head of the company as follows:

"I came into this company to preside over its death, but instead I decided I could save it," he said. "I'm the first person since Cyrus

Curtis himself who's been both the chief executive and the chief stockholder, and so I've had the kind of authority you have to have in order to make vital decisions.[121]

The Revival of the Magazine

SerVaas said that he had decided to reactivate the *Post* in the spring of 1971 as a 200-page quarterly, directed toward the "middle American," on the basis of significant financial improvements in the Curtis Company and his own "nostalgia" for the magazine. In the 22 months since the magazine ceased publishing, the company had received over a million letters from people asking, as SerVaas put it, "Why did you stop? Why? The *Post* was more America than anything."[122]

SerVaas obviously arrived at a successful formula. He had turned the reborn *Post* into a modest success. The new edition contained many of the old editorial features, and the only up-to-date aspect was its price, a steep $1 per copy.[123]

The first two issues sold out their 500,000 copy press run, and the third issue was increased to 550,000. The SerVaas publishing style was unorthodox in that his wife, a physician, with no previous experience in the general-interest magazine field, served as executive editor, and his daughter and niece did some editing of the magazine.[124]

By July 1973, it was obvious that SerVaas had succeeded in resuscitating the *Post*. The magazine was not dying. It had been dead for two-and-one-half years when he resurrected it in June 1971, as a quarterly. Two years later it was being published six times a year, and its publisher reported plans for nine issues in 1974 and monthly publication in 1975. He also stated that it had a circulation of 800,000 and was making money.[125]

As this chapter is concluded a remark attributed to Cary Bok, grandson of the founder of the Curtis Publishing Company and former director of the corporation, comes to mind: "The real history of the *Saturday Evening Post* is going to have to be written by a psychiatrist."[126]

NOTES

1. Letter by D. J. Kelly, Jr., in the D. J. Kelly, Jr., "Collection of Early Historical Newspapers," May 5, 1946. See Appendix B.

2. Frank Luther Mott, *A History of American Magazines*, 5 vols. (Cambridge: Harvard University Press, 1957), vol. 4, p. 674.

3. Ibid., pp. 675, 676, 677.

4. The Curtis Publishing Company, *A Short History of The Saturday Evening Post* (Philadelphia: The Curtis Publishing Company, 1937), p. 9.

5. Ibid., pp. 10-11.

6. Ibid., p. 11.

7. James Playsted Wood, *The Curtis Magazines* (New York: The Ronald Press Company, 1971), p. 50.

8. Ibid., p. 51.

9. Theodore Bernard Peterson, "Consumer Magazines in the United States, 1900-1950" (Ph.D. diss., University of Illinois, 1955), p. 34.

10. Frank Presbrey, *The History and Development of Advertising* (Garden City, N.Y.: Doubleday, Dorn and Company, 1929), p. 471.

11. The Curtis Publishing Company, *Short History*, p. 11.

12. Mott, *History*, vol. 4, pp. 684-85.

13. Ibid., vol. 4, p. 691.

14. Ibid., vol. 4, pp. 694-96.

15. The Curtis Publishing Company, *Short History*, p. 13.

16. Isaac Marcosson, *Before I Forget* (New York: Dodd, Mead and Company, 1959), p. 30.

17. Wood, *Curtis Magazines*, p. 95.

18. Ibid., p. 11.

19. The Curtis Publishing Company, *Short History*, pp. 11, 12.

20. Wood, *Magazines*, pp. 124-25.

21. Ibid., p. 126.

22. Mott, *History*, vol. 4, p. 699.

23. Ibid.

24. Ibid.

25. Peterson, "Consumer Magazines," p. 23

26. Wood, *Curtis Magazines*, p. 69.

27. James Playsted Wood, *Magazines in the United States*, 2nd ed. (New York: The Ronald Press Company, 1956), p. 154.

28. Personal Interview with John Caples, vice-president, Batten, Barton, Durstine & Osborn, Inc., New York, New York, December 7, 1977.

29. Presbey, *History*, p. 471.

30. Wood, *Magazines*, p. 134.

31. Ibid., p. 139.

32. Ibid., p. 140.

33. Curtis Publishing Company file, 1960.

34. Wood, *Magazines*, p. 143.

35. Peterson, "Consumer Magazines," p. 23.

36. Ibid., p. 27.

37. Ibid., p. 28.

38. Curtis Publishing Company file, October 1949.

39. Ibid.

40. Ibid.

41. Ibid.

42. Ibid.

43. Ibid.

44. "Curtis' Net Earnings," *Tide* (October 14, 1949), p. 30.

45. Michael J. Saada, "Magazine Rate Increase," *Wall Street Journal*, October 11, 1947, p. 1.

46. Ibid.

47. Ibid.

48. Ibid.

49. Wood, *Magazines*, pp. 146-47.

50. Ibid.

51. Ibid., p. 148.

52. Ibid., p. 153.

53. The Curtis Publishing Company, *Short History*, p. 30.

54. Ibid.

55. Curtis Publishing Company file, 1960.

56. Wood, *Magazines*, p. 164.

57. Ibid., p. 174.

58. Curtis Publishing Company file, 1960.

59. Ibid.

60. Wood, *Magazines*, p. 212.

61. Curtis Publishing Company, *Short History*, p. 45.

62. Wood, *Magazines*, p. 194.

63. Ibid., p. 243.

64. John M. Lee, "Curtis Publishing Has a New Format" *New York Times*, April, 1962, p. 1.

65. Ibid., p. 10.

66. "View From the 9th Floor," *Newsweek* (April 2, 1962), p. 62.

67. Ibid.

68. Ibid.

69. Curtis Publishing Company file, March, 1962.

70. Mathew J. Culligan, *The Curtis-Culligan Story* (New York: Crown Publishers, Inc., 1970), pp. 42, 43.

71. Ibid.

72. Wood, *Magazines*, p. 257.

73. "*Post's* Death Haunts Him," *Advertising Age* (January 26, 1970), p. 1.

74. Wood, *Magazines*, p. 261.

75. Culligan, *Curtis-Culligan Story*, p. 73.

76. "Culligan's Round," *Newsweek* (December 23, 1963), p. 69.

77. Ibid.

78. "Magazine Publisher Sees Brighter Days," *Detroit News*, April 4, 1963, p. 1.

79. Curtis Publishing Company News Release, August 31, 1964.

80. Wood, *Magazines*, p. 262.

81. Ibid.

82. Culligan, *Curtis-Culligan Story*, pp. 131-32.

83. Wood, *Magazines*, p. 264.

84. Culligan, *Curtis-Culligan Story*, pp. 169-71. See Appendix D.

85. Otto Friedrich, *Decline and Fall* (New York: Harper & Row, 1970), p. 65.

86. Ibid., p. 68.

87. Ibid., p. 50.

88. Harvard Business School, *The Saturday Evening Post*, Case History, Number 6-373-009, 1972, p. 17.

89. Ibid., p. 140.

90. *New York Times*, October 11, 1964, p. 1.

91. Wood, *Magazines*, p. 266.

92. A. Kent MacDougal, "*Saturday Evening Post* After a Long and Stormy Search for a New Image," *Wall Street Journal*, November 16, 1964, p. 4.

93. Ibid.

94. Culligan, *Curtis-Culligan Story*, p. 190.

95. Ibid., pp. 193-94.

96. Culligan, *Curtis-Culligan Story*, p. 195.

97. Wood, *Magazines*, p. 266.

98. Chris Welles, "*Post*-Mortem," *New York* (February 10, 1969), p. 32.

99. Ibid.

100. Ibid., p. 33.

101. "New Bundle of Hope for Ailing *Post*," *Business Week* (May 25, 1968), p. 42.

102. Ibid.

103. Ibid.

104. Ibid.

105. "Time Inc. to Lend Curtis Publishing Co. $5 Million and Give it Other Assistance," *The Wall Street Journal*, May 20, 1968, p. 1.

106. "Special '*Post*' for Execs Tells Circulation Plan," *Advertising Age* (June 10, 1968), p. 1.

107. Personal Interview with Stephen E. Kelly, former publisher of *The Saturday Evening Post*, April 1, 1977.

108. "Curtis Sales Staffs United," *Wall Street Journal*, August 23, 1968, p. 1.

109. Friedrich, *Decline*, pp. 342, 343. Emphasis in original.

110. Ibid., p. 352.

111. Ibid., p. 353.

112. Chris Welles, "*Post*-Mortem," p. 33.

113. Ibid., pp. 33-34.

114. Ibid., p. 36.

115. Robert E. Bedingfield, "Feb. 8 Issue of *Saturday Evening Post* to be Last," *New York Times*, January 11, 1969, p. 1.

116. Ibid.

117. Robert E. Bedingfield, "Two Directors Quit at Curtis and *Post*," *New York Times*, February 13, 1969, p. 1.

118. Friedrich, *Decline*, p. 469.

119. Ibid., pp. 472, 473.

120. Herbert D. Maneloveg, "*Post* Gives Lesson in How Not to Market a Magazine," *Advertising Age* (February 10, 1969), p. 56. Emphasis in original.

121. Lacey Fosburgh, "*Saturday Evening Post* to Reappear as a Quarterly," *New York Times*, November 6, 1970, p. 47.

122. Ibid.

123. "The Good Old Ways," *Newsweek* (December 13, 1971), p. 74.

124. Ibid.

125. Philip H. Dougherty, "Curtis Turns Over an Old Leaf," *New York Times*, July 8, 1973, p. 15.

126. Joseph Goulden, *The Curtis Caper* (New York: G. P. Putnam's Sons, 1965), p. 11.

6

BETTER HOMES AND GARDENS

EDWIN T. MEREDITH, SR.

Edwin T. Meredith, Sr., published the first issue of *Successful Farming* in October 1902. This event marked the beginning of Meredith Corporation which, along with its first publication, now produces *Better Homes and Gardens* (*BH&G*), *Apartment Life*, and special interest publications.[1]

The second magazine to be originated by Meredith was one he had assigned staff members to investigate, resurrecting an idea he had been considering for several years. Believing that a service magazine similar to *Successful Farming* could be marketed, he launched *Fruit, Garden and Home*, on June 1, 1922. Meredith had described his new venture:

> Eventually *Fruit, Garden and Home* will have as large a circulation as *Successful Farming*. It is designed to meet a need in the magazine field. We have national magazines for the well-to-do family in town and country, but no paper for the average city or country establishment. The new publication will circulate in both city and country.[2]

When the magazine was launched, advertisers were paying $1 for each line and $450 for each black and white page. For $900 the advertiser could have blue or black and two other colors. In contrast, the well-established *Successful Farming* had a black and white page rate of $1,800 and a three-color rate of $2,475.[3]

Fruit, Garden and Home was not a profitable venture. In 1924 the name was changed to *Better Homes and Gardens*. It was not until 1927 that it began to show a profit.

Better Homes and Gardens

Meredith himself went East to sell advertising for the first issue of the newly named magazine, and guaranteed a circulation of 150,000. By 1925 a single black and white advertising page in *BH&G* sold for $1,800, a four-color second and third cover sold for $3,000, and a fourth cover, or back page, was $3,600.[4]

At the time of Meredith's death in 1928, *BH&G* and *Successful Farming* had reached a combined circulation of 2.5 million. Under the leadership of publisher Fred O. Bohen, Meredith's son-in-law, the magazine continued its growth.[5] After World War II the magazine's advertising linage grew to the point where it passed such magazines as *McCall's*, *Good Housekeeping*, and *Ladies' Home Journal*, to become the advertising linage leader among monthly magazines. By this time it was guaranteeing advertisers a circulation of one million.[6]

In 1968 magazine historian Frank Luther Mott attributed much of the success of *BH&G* to " . . . resourceful business management, as well as to the fact that the magazine had been consistently faithful editorially to its original ideals."[7]

E. T. Meredith was one of the first magazine publishers to realize the management advantage of forming executive committees to meet on policy matters governing the business aspects of a magazine. He formed the conference which was made up of heads of all major departments including printing and mailing. These executives met regularly on Friday mornings, and when necessary, to discuss company affairs. Meredith relied on the conference to air opinions about the business and to ensure executive accord when decisions were to be implemented.[8]

Sales Promotion

Many of the promotional ideas that later were to be responsible for much of the success of *BH&G* were started at *Successful Farming*. By 1912 the parent company had expanded several times, and operations were moved to 1716 Locust Street in Des Moines, Iowa, where the main company office remains today. There were more than 200 employees at that time, and they were engaged in dozens of circulation and promotion schemes, many of which involved the readers in contests as well as subscription sales.[9]

It was during a summer sales meeting in Des Moines in 1924 that the title *Better Homes and Gardens* was announced as the new name of *Fruit, Garden and Home.* The August 1924 issue was the first to bear the new name and logotype.[10]

The *BH&G* formula for success was built on service to the settled, middle-class, American husband and wife whose main interests were their home and family. There was nothing new in the idea of service to the reader. Since the days of Edward Bok, of Curtis fame, magazines had tried to relate their content to the readers' lives and experiences.[11]

With the first issue under the new name the readers were recipients of a periodical of 50 pages, with large illustrations and a circulation of half a million. By 1928, at the time of Meredith's death, it was a prosperous-looking monthly, with some issues of more than 150 pages, and it had reached the one million mark in circulation— the first magazine in history to achieve that goal without the aid of fiction or fashions.[12]

Service to Readers

In the magazine's early issues, Meredith established his editorial credo: "Service is what it's all about—service is the secret."[13] He ruled out fiction from the start, temporarily silencing critics with his jingle, "No piffle, no passion; no fiction, no fashion,"[14] and permanently silencing them with his promotional success. He pioneered in the how-to editorial approach and introduced the *BH&G* advertising guarantee. He saw the magazine achieve one million circulation in the year of his death. Salesman, organizer, editor, and advertising man, he built a solid foundation for the publication and passed on his vision and enthusiasm for the magazine.[15]

FRED O. BOHEN

Fred O. Bohen, who became the new company head in 1928, had joined the Chicago office as an advertising sales representative for *Successful Farming* in 1921. He moved to Des Moines in 1923, and served four years as advertising director for both *Successful Farming* and *BH&G*, before being named general manager of the company in 1927. He became publisher in 1928 and president and chairman of the board in 1929.

Under Bohen's leadership, *BH&G* grew into one of the nation's leading magazines. Circulation went from 1 million to nearly 7.5

million between 1928 and 1968. Yearly advertising revenue climbed from $2 million to nearly $37 million in the same period.[16]

During those years, Bohen's personal calls on advertisers took him from coast to coast. He solicited advertising accounts himself, accompanying his salesmen. He developed close friendships with top-level advertising and agency men across the country through active memberships in groups like the National Association of Manufacturers, Business Advisory Council to the President, and the board of directors of the Audit Bureau of Circulations.[17]

Bohen guided *BH&G* and the company through the critical Depression. While the magazine was experiencing growing pains, he secured bank financing. He also instituted postwar planning, including investments in new printing equipment, building additions, and paper contracts, all of which helped *BH&G* move ahead of competitors at the end of the war. For nearly 40 years, Bohen was the chief executive for the magazine and the Meredith Publishing Company.[18]

First Cookbook

Like the magazine's founder, Bohen never missed an opportunity to expound *BH&G*'s virtues, nearly making a religion out of the how-to doctrine.

Before *My Better Homes and Gardens Cook Book* rolled off the presses in 1930, Bohen challenged, "If you can't produce the best in its field, scrap the idea."[19] Editors rose to the occasion, and the cookbook soon became instrumental in selling food advertising for the magazine, as well as a best seller in its own right. Rex Starr, a member of the promotion department, originated the idea to sell the magazine with a premium and the premium was the cookbook.[20] Bohen also stimulated publication of the first idea annuals and the growth of reader research.

THE GREAT DEPRESSION

The Great Depression seems to have stimulated the management to enterprise in developing new projects. Publication of *My Better Homes and Gardens Cook Book* in 1930 gave Meredith a new distinction in that field. Cookbooks have always ranked high among nonliterary best sellers in the United States. This book reached a total of ten million in sales in 1964, greater than any other American hardcover book; among top long-term best sellers in the United States. At that time it had been exceeded only by the Bible.[21]

It was also in 1930 that the magazine promoted a comprehensive national home-building plan, including the establishment of standards, long-time amortization of costs, and a national association to determine loan risks for such projects. By 1930 the Junior Garden Clubs, which had been promoted by *BH&G* the preceding year, were flourishing; they later reached a membership of half a million.[22]

E. T. Meredith, Jr., returned from the University of Virginia to assist in the company his father had founded. He worked in many divisions of the company, including advertising offices in New York and Chicago. In 1935 he returned to Des Moines as vice-president, treasurer, and general manager.[23]

A COLOR REVOLUTION

At the end of the Depression in 1937, the management began to foresee a color revolution developing in printing that would affect advertising and editorial matter. Pressroom supervisors were sent to many different plants to inspect color equipment and make recommendations to the management. Two four-color presses were finally ordered.[24]

Color, especially four-color, was limited to the editorial pages. This new color equipment improved operations and furnished the advertising representatives with new incentive to sell advertising pages printed in color, but World War II started before the company could realize significant monetary returns on the equipment investment. At the same time that the color presses were put into operation, the magazine shifted to a larger page size measuring 9-1/2 inches by 12-1/2 inches, or 680 agate lines, a better known advertising page measurement.[25] Thirty-two years later, the Meredith Corporation invested extensively in the color printing business, and in July 1969, formed Meredith/Burda Corporation of Lynchburg, Virginia, a merger that resulted in one of the leading rotogravure printing plants in the United States.[26]

WORLD WAR II PERIOD

In 1938 Frank W. McDonough became editor of *BH&G* and held the position through the 1940s. The years of World War II brought shortages of paper and also a reduction in advertising caused by the use, by the armed services, of materials commonly employed in the manufacture of goods offered to the public. *BH&G* became a leader in the Victory Gardens movement. In 1943 it helped to meet the "war baby" surge and the shortage of doctors by issuing its *Baby Book*, which was to sell a million and a half copies within the next decade.[27]

Advertising revenue dropped off about $1 million in the first year of the United States participation in the war, which meant a 25 percent loss. The advertising linage came back in the next year largely with the aid of liberal food-advertising—a field in which *BH&G* had always done well. Immediately after the war, through vigorous efforts, largely centered upon techniques of cooperation with dealers in construction materials, department stores, and house furnishing retailers (most of them originated in earlier years but now pursued with increased energy), *BH&G* recovered from its slump. It proceeded to overtake the *Woman's Home Companion*, *McCall's*, *Good Housekeeping*, and the *Ladies' Home Journal* in total advertising receipts by the beginning of the 1950s. Though it kept this primacy for a few years, it eventually lost it in the shifts of competition; it did continue to retain a position near the top of the magazines published for women and the home, in both circulation and advertising.[28]

The advent of World War II brought restrictions on the production of consumer goods, travel, printing paper, and manpower, This created frustrating problems in every phase of the magazine's operations. Priorities on transportation facilities often put carloads of copies of the magazine on railroad sidings in order that strategic materials could be moved.[29]

Diversification

Following his discharge from the U.S. Navy in 1945 as a lieutenant commander, E. T. Meredith, Jr., returned to the company and was instrumental in leading it into commercial broadcasting. In a race to be included in the first 50 original licensed television stations, Meredith actually constructed a station in 90 days—WHEN in Syracuse, New York. In 1951, 1952, and 1960 the company purchased WOW in Omaha, KPHO in Phoenix, and KCMO in Kansas City, respectively.[30]

As *BH&G* grew, emphasis on various subjects shifted somewhat. Initially, the magazine regarded gardens, inspirational homemaking, and building as its most important subjects. By 1931 articles were departmentalized under gardens, foods and recipes, building, and home management.

Building, remodeling, and home furnishing articles increased, while space given to gardening remained relatively unchanged. As early as 1945, "and Gardens" on the magazine's cover began appearing in smaller type.

One of the magazine's major changes in editorial emphasis occurred during World War II. On all editorial subjects affected by the war, and that included most, *BH&G* demonstrated a new kind of creativity. A major portion of editorial space previously devoted to landscaping and flower gardening was now concerned with vegetable growing—Victory Gardens.

Research

Early research conducted for the publication usually centered on the readership of advertisements. Frank R. Furbush joined Meredith's research department in 1932, and was named acting research director in 1942. He was elected a vice-president in 1961 and placed in charge of research activities. In 1968 he became director of corporate planning, the post he held until his retirement in September 1975.[31]

Furbush realized the value of setting up research projects that would indicate the magazine's closeness to its readers. Mills Shepherd and Daniel Starch, outside research organizations, were employed to investigate these aspects of the magazine's influence.[32]

POSTWAR EXPANSION

During the period 1946-1954, advertising revenue increased a substantial 172 percent. It jumped from $8,737,868 in 1946 to $23,741,055 in 1954. *BH&G* topped all other major monthly magazines in advertising pages and revenue in 1954.[33]

Innovations

In the April 1955 issue, Reynolds Metals Company ran a full-color advertisement in the magazine on aluminum foil laminated to paper, the first such advertisement to appear in a major consumer magazine. The cost of the Reynolds spread was $135,000, including foil. This was one of the revolutionary innovations which have continued to be a *BH&G* stock-in-trade.[34]

In 1937 the punched recipe pages, which insert into the best-selling *Better Homes and Gardens New Cook Book*, were another *BH&G* first.

A Record-Breaking Issue

The April 1953 issue broke many records. With 416 pages, it was, and still is, the biggest issue of *BH&G* ever published in number of pages. This issue also set a new high among all magazines, with advertising revenue of $4,495,000.[35]

After some lean years following the 1958-59 recession, *BH&G* began a string of seven consecutive years of gains in advertising revenue, going from $21,259,683 in 1963 to $38,929,292 in 1969.[36]

In 1951 the magazine began the presentation of its advertising guarantee in a graphic form, recognizable as a symbol. In 1963 the symbol was made available to *BH&G* advertisers for use in general promotion and advertising. It was prominently displayed by this time in connection with the magazine's mail order advertising, a department of small illustrated "ads" begun in 1933 under the heading "It's News to Me" and later entitled "Gift Shopping by Mail."[37]

During the years 1957-1961, Meredith Corporation undertook a physical expansion program that cost over $10 million. Although the publishing plant in Des Moines had been extended and remodeled from time to time in preceding years, a new printing plant was built, covering about ten acres and equipped with modern high-speed, six-color presses. Its facilities enabled the company to publish not only *BH&G* and *Successful Farming*, but also other magazines on a contract printing basis.

Regional Advertising

Regional advertising was a relatively new and important development in the magazine industry. Because of its outstanding printing facilities, in 1972 *BH&G* was unmatched in regional advertising flexibility. An advertiser could buy a geographical region, a state (or a combination of states), test markets, or one or more of 55 top markets (metropolitan areas). He could use the *BH&G* Super Spot Edition, if he were interested in reaching 1.1 million families living in high-income zip zones. Or he could reach 800,000 *BH&G* families who had just changed addresses in the Movers' Edition. Two Travel Directories also were available: Travel Director East, with 1.2 million circulation on the eastern seaboard, and Western Travel Director, which went to 1.3 million *BH&G* families living in 13 western states.[38]

The biggest regional advertising year in the magazine's history was 1971—$8,540,245 (19.2 percent of total revenue). An average of

159 different regional editions for each issue was published. In contrast, total regional ad revenue in 1963 was $2,888,381, and the average number of editions was 19 for each issue. In 1972 three consecutive million-dollar-plus regional advertising issues were published in March, April, and May. With $1,247,875, May 1972 was the largest regional revenue issue BH&G had produced to date.[39]

The Postwar Period

Bohen and his management team searched thoroughly for ways to use postwar profits to enhance the company's competitive position. In 1945 the magazine began its nationwide Home Planning Service program, which was featured in leading department stores and financial institutions throughout the country. More than a million families had made use of the service by September 1947, and in July 1947, the magazine was presented with the American Public Relations Association's top award for the most "meritorious public relations performance in the field of publication."[40]

Mott summed up this journalistic performance:

> The great distinguishing characteristic of this magazine was the precise practicality, this usable service for house, home, and family. Of course this was not a new concept for home magazines, but *Better Homes and Gardens* worked harder at it than had any of the others. Men leaving the staff of the Des Moines magazine carried this policy and its techniques to other publications, and thus Meredith exerted a special influence on the entire field of home magazines at the mid-century.[41]

In 1954 a 12-month study was undertaken for the publication by Alfred Politz Research. More than 25,000 personal interviews were completed during the year, and 5,448 of the 7,512 respondents contacted were interviewed four times to study continued interest in the magazine. The average readership for each issue at the time was 15,550,000, almost four persons for each copy of the magazine.[42]

Over the years, many other magazines followed BH&G's lead in forming their own research departments, and advertisers became confused in the volume of findings projected by the different publications. As a result, BH&G, like other magazines today, shares syndicated research findings of the Simmons and Starch surveys. These unbiased research organizations put publications on "equal ground" and allowed BH&G's research staff to pursue more specialized studies.[43]

The editorial in the 25th-anniversary issue, published in September 1947, outlined the philosophy of the publication. Writing under the title, "Your Home Is Where Our Heart Is," the editor said:

> But our interest is the family; and all the penetrating analyses and solemn warnings in the world don't lift a finger toward holding the family together. Nor can an unhappy family be made happy by law. At least we don't think so.
>
> That is why in *Better Homes and Gardens* in all our 25 years you've never seen any wringings of the hands. It's not because we sometimes haven't felt like it or that we're not aware that it's "good copy," man being the morbid creature he is, but rather because it does no good.
>
> Instead, our purpose has been quietly to stimulate new interests, new richness to hold together the family and home. You don't stop a boy from idling on the street corner by haranguing him. You help him set up a workshop and build a canoe in the basement instead. You don't keep a girl out of the back seat with horrified descriptions of the pit. You roll up the living-room rug for a dance.[44]

The 256-page 25th-anniversary issue set an all-time high record in the number of pages, color inserts, and advertising linage.[45]

Advertising Growth

Since its first issue, *BH&G* has been able to offer prospective advertisers a unique editorial philosophy based on home and family service, plus a sound circulation policy. In 1922, its first year of existence, it garnered $23,744 in advertising revenue. By the end of its first full year (1923) the advertising revenue was nearly $157,000. By the end of 1926 it topped $1 million for the first time. In 1929, the year of the Wall Street crash, it was at an all-time high of $2,690,788.[46]

During the 1930s the vitality and potency of their 100 percent home and family service formula and several editorial innovations, backed by promotional programs, brought major new advertisers to the magazine. By the end of 1937 the Depression was over, and the American economy was beginning to recover. Advertising revenue topped.$3 million for the first time that year.[47]

By 1940 *BH&G* emerged as a real contender with other major magazines. It entered the charmed circle of the top ten circulation magazines, and advertisers invested a record $3,983,594. There was a drop-off during the World War II years, followed by a steady increase in revenue from $4,149,244 in 1943 to $76,334,532 in 1977.[48]

FIFTIETH ANNIVERSARY

Although the year 1972 marked the 50th anniversary of the founding of the magazine, its management and editors took a somewhat stoic approach to the event. In their opinion, readers and advertisers really didn't care about the company's age or its mellowing history.

As Wayne Miller, vice-president and general manager of Meredith's Magazine Division, stated:

> *Better Homes and Gardens* is taking a low-key, business-like approach to its 50th anniversary, using the occasion to look at the magazine as it is today and to assess its future. We're too busy planning for tomorrow to take much more than a brief look at the past.[49]

The circulation department did capitalize on the 50-year theme in a special golden anniversary direct mail package. Instead of looking back, the package promoted what the magazine had to offer in 1972. It went to millions of prospective *BH&G* readers. The annual sales conference of the magazine celebrated the occasion by holding its meeting in the 50th state at the island of Maui in Hawaii. The theme of the conference was the forecast of $50 million in revenue in the publication's 50th year.[50]

More on Research

During another attempt at research, the magazine made a survey early in 1968 and received 278,477 responses to a long questionnaire. From these, the magazine selected, at random, 5,000 replies for tabulating.

More than half the respondents were deeply concerned and wanted effective measures to control inflation and another 37 percent were worried but "... didn't know what to recommend."[51] As to the role of government in combating inflation, another question elicited that only 10 percent believed the administration was taking strong enough measures to halt it.[52]

When it came to increasing community services, the respondents indicated a strong dislike for new and higher income taxes or higher property taxes. Instead, they preferred new or higher sales taxes, increased corporation taxes, or a reduction of community services. At the same time, they believed that the lower-income groups were hit most unfairly by income taxes. One result of their pessimism was that 54 percent believed that they could about stay even in relation to rising living costs during the next five years, and 20 percent thought their income would fall behind in the cost of living race.[53]

In 1976 the magazine contacted advertisers to announce its new research service that would enable marketers to receive information on a variety of consumer attitudes and issues, test out a recipe, or even sample a new product.

BH&G's Consumer Panel consisted of 1,000 households gleaned from the publication's subscribers, representative of its circulation, demographically and geographically. Each month, beginning in March 1976, a questionnaire of some 15 pages covering several broad areas was sent to the panel members. The first month's questions, for example, were on consumer confidence, shopping habits, and supermarkets. Marketers could suggest questions for inclusion in the list. Data were cross-tabulated with demographic information and supplied to the marketer free of charge. The magazine said the service was open to advertisers and nonadvertisers. For out-of-pocket costs only, a company was able to use the consumer panel to test out a recipe or a new product. Paul Stuempfig, research director, stated that coupons to be used for the purchase of recipe ingredients or a sample of a new entry were mailed out to panel members for their appraisal. He said the service " . . . won't be used for anything but strict research . . .";[54] there would be no promoting of any products. All advertiser requests and samplings were kept confidential; names of panel members were not disclosed. For their assistance in the service, panel members received points that could be redeemed for a variety of premiums, mostly BH&G hardcover books.[55]

Long-time Leading Advertisers

Of the ten advertisers with the largest total expenditure in BH&G during 1971, eight had been advertising in the magazine for 30 years or more. These eight are indicated by an asterisk in the list that follows:[56]

1. General Mills* $1,930,804
2. General Foods* 1,783,851
3. Sears 1,561,951
4. Procter & Gamble* 1,334,530
5. Armstrong Cork* 1,099,710
6. Pillsbury* 871,237
7. Kraftco* 781,200
8. Norton Simon 716,851
9. Lever Brothers* 694,744
10. General Motors* 686,800

Among other important companies which have advertised in *BH&G* for 30 years or more, and which used the magazine in 1972, the 50th-anniversary year, were: American Home Products, Borden, Campbell's Soup, Dole, Del Monte, General Electric, Hormel, Kimberly-Clark, National Biscuit, Scott Paper, and Sterling Drug.[57]

Circulation Growth

Subscriptions made up approximately 90 percent of *BH&G's* circulation total in the early years, with direct mail advertising the primary source of subscription sales. Through direct mail the magazine was offered to a carefully selected segment of the national market.

BH&G subscribers were perhaps some of the magazine's best promoters. In 1923 E. T. Meredith encouraged subscribers to go after new *BH&G* readers. In a publisher's letter, Meredith asked readers to get subscriptions from friends and neighbors, so circulation promotion funds could go " . . . for extra editorial features each month."[58] Readers continued in later years to sell *BH&G*, according to management, but much less obviously—through gift subscriptions, passing along copies of the magazine, and recommending its editorial content.[59]

In addition to subscriptions, approximately 700,000 copies of *BH&G* were sold over newsstands across the country every month. In the magazine's first full year, newsstand sales averaged just over 13,000 copies each month. Sales hit a peak in 1953, averaging 1.5 million copies each month. During the period 1968-1972 sales leveled off and averaged 600,000 to 700,000 copies each month.[60]

The magazine started with a charter circulation of 150,000. The first two issues were published on a trial basis and sent without charge to subscribers. Regular subscription rates of 35 cents a year, or $1 for three years went into effect in September 1923. By this time, with the magazine little more than a year old, circulation reached over 300,000. Reception to the magazine had been enthusiastic.[61]

By midyear 1924, *BH&G* reached one-half million in circulation. Subscriptions went up to 60 cents a year, or $1 for two years. This increase in subscription price marked the end of the magazine's experimental period. With the magazine showing a healthy growth, E. T. Meredith told readers, "*BH&G* is going to be the most potent influence for good that the American home has."[62]

Four years later, circulation hit one million. Following Meredith's death in 1928, circulation grew to an average of 1.5 million a month in the next ten years. With the beginning of the 1940s it passed the 2 million copies each month mark, and became one of the top ten magazines in circulation.

During the war years that followed, paper shortages hampered circulation growth. But the end of the war brought a turning point. From 1946 to 1954 circulation soared, breaking one record after another. Over 1 million more families became *BH&G* families. The September 1952 issue carried the announcement that the magazine was now serving more than 3.5 million.

On the second anniversary of its birth, *BH&G's* editor wrote: "When *Better Homes and Gardens* was launched, we had in mind that it must be a magazine that would attract and be helpful to at least 1 million subscribers."[63] By 1963 in the forty-first year, circulation totaled over six million. Subscriptions were selling for $3 a year, and the magazine was well on its way toward a 2.5 million monthly circulation gain between 1960 and 1970. *BH&G* opened the 1970s with a guaranteed average monthly circulation of 7,777,777. The magazine remained at that unusual 7's guarantee for two years. In 1977 the magazine reached 8,044,168 in total average monthly circulation.[64]

MORTON S. BAILEY, JR.

Morton S. Bailey, Jr., was named publisher of *BH&G* in 1969. Before that he had served as advertising director. His father held the position of advertising director of the *Saturday Evening Post* in 1957, at the time of his death. Bailey was quoted as stating: "My dad was one of the few who saw trouble coming, and I think it killed him."[65] At the same time he remarked: "I'd be tickled to death if our young son, John, decided this was the business he wanted."[66]

It was only three years after declaring his enthusiasm for the magazine that Bailey resigned, effective January 31, 1972, to join *Ladies' Home Journal* as advertising director. He moved into a post vacated when Louis Porterfield became the publisher in October 1971.[67]

Bailey's duties at *BH&G* were assumed by Jack D. Rehm, group publishing director for Meredith. Rehm said at the time that no permanent publisher would be named in the immediate future.[68]

A 23-year *BH&G* veteran, and publisher since 1969, Bailey was described by a company source as having been increasingly dissatisfied with his New York-based job ever since a company reorganization about a year and a half before.

Bailey praised *BH&G* as a "very fine" publication when contacted by *Advertising Age*, but noted that "irreconcilable differences" led to his resignation. Sources noted that Bailey initiated contact with *Ladies' Home Journal* where Porterfield was involved in a search for his own successor. Rehm would say only that Bailey's departure was amicable.[69]

Image Stressing

The publication's management decided in February 1973 to launch an advertising promotional campaign through a new agency, in which it positioned itself as a professional journal. "It's the world's largest professional journal if the homemaker is a professional," [70] said Kenneth E. Olshan, executive vice-president of John Rockwell & Associates.

The first advertisement's headline read: "23 Million People Read a Magazine With No News, No Entertainment, No Gossip, No Sex."[71] Rehm said: "We're pretty dull and unexciting unless you're looking for better ways to run a home. . . . Everything we talk about is close to home."[72]

ROBERT A. BURNETT

In December 1975, Meredith Corporation announced plans to spend $23 million on a modernization program that included conversion of *BH&G* to a smaller page size.

According to Robert A. Burnett, president, the program was financed by $23 million in loans. Of the total, $15 million was obtained from private lenders and the remaining $8 million from banks. The loan from private lenders was to have been repaid over 15 years, with the bank loans coming due in 1980.[73]

BH&G's advertising sales suffered during the 1975 recession. Advertising pages were 875.1, a decline of almost 16 percent from the previous year. In the spring of 1976, in an effort to correct the situation, it began soliciting cigarette advertising for the first time in five years. In 1976 it carried 16.5 pages of advertisements for smoking materials.[74]

The magazine also announced it would raise its subscription price from $6 to $8 early in 1977 to help defray higher postal costs. It said it would expand use of a private delivery service in San Francisco and begin using a similar service in Chicago in February 1977.[75]

Burnett, president and chief executive officer of Meredith Corporation, joined the publishing company in 1952 as a member of the advertising sales department of *BH&G*. He served successively as a sales analyst, sales representative, Cleveland sales manager, marketing manager, and in 1961 was appointed advertising director of the magazine. In 1965 he was elected a vice-president of the company and served as publisher of *BH&G* from 1966 until May 1973, when he was appointed president and chief operating officer. The board of directors elected him to his present position in February 1977. He has had operating responsibility for the company's three divisions: publishing, printing, and broadcasting.[76]

BH&G and the Meredith Corporation have every intention of progressing in the years ahead to even greater heights. Burnett made this quite clear in the interview.

> We believe a stagnant business is a dying business. Meredith Corporation must continue to grow through expansion of existing businesses, acquisitions and internally developed new business opportunities. Successful organizations quite often don't explode. They grow carefully, steadily and the alternative, of course, is to become senile and to decay. I am a believer in self-renewal, the alternative of which is self-decay. *Better Homes and Gardens* is one of the greatest examples of a self-renewing product that I could ever find. . . . that self-renewal came as a result of determined and dedicated effort on the part of editors who understand innovation. We are going to go to maybe $500,000,000 in 1985. We are at $235,000,000 now. It involves 2,000 pages of advertising for *BH&G* and $100,000 in advertising revenue.[77]

Sound management and business practices are as essential to the successful operation of a magazine as to any other business enterprise. *BH&G* has been a successful operation almost from the beginning. One of the reasons could well be the fact that they promote their executives from within the company, witness Rehm and Burnett, among others. During the author's interviews at the company personally, and on the phone to Des Moines, an excellent state of morale could be detected, both among the top executives and division managers.

BH&G and Meredith have, for many years, exercised an attitude of social and community involvement that has reaped rewards which are probably incalculable. For instance, for years Meredith professionals have been sharing their knowledge of communications with various members of the educational community in and around Des Moines, Iowa, home of the company headquarters. Early in 1976 a new development was launched, when Dr. Herbert Strentz, dean of

Drake University's School of Journalism, met with James Riggs, Meredith's vice-president for new product development. The result was a one-semester seminar organized and presented entirely by Meredith Corporation people. The course, J-175 or Magazine Publishing Management, involved 25 Meredith specialists who lectured at various times during the semester. Dr. Strentz stated: "The course has been a significant addition to the curriculum, offering students insights and instruction that simply are not available elsewhere."[78]

The publishing firm believes that its most valuable asset has been its employees and the knowledge each possesses. Sharing that resource with those wishing to learn is a responsibility that the firm has readily assumed.[79]

NOTES

1. Personal Interview with Jack D. Rehm, publisher of *Better Homes and Gardens*, New York, New York, December 9, 1977.

2. "Meredith Starts a New Magazine," *Des Moines Register*, April 13, 1922, p. 1.

3. Larry Kai Ebert, "Meredith at 75," *Advertising Age* (October 31, 1977), p. 78.

4. Theodore Peterson, *Magazines in the Twentieth Century*, 2nd ed. (Urbana: University of Illinois Press, 1964), p. 384.

5. Personal Interview with Otto G. Schaefer, former New York advertising director, *BH&G*, Scarsdale, New York, July 3, 1978.

6. Ibid.

7. Frank L. Mott, *A History of American Magazines*, 5 vols. (Cambridge: Harvard University Press, 1968), vol. 5, p. 48.

8. Carol Reuss, "*Better Homes and Gardens* and its Editors" (Ph.D. diss., The University of Iowa, 1970), p. 19.

9. Ibid., p. 9.

10. Peterson, *Magazines*, p. 382.

11. Ibid.

12. Mott, *History*, vol. 5, p. 38.

13. *BH&G*, 1 (July 1922), p. 3.

14. Ibid.

15. Ibid.

16. *BH&G* file, October 1928.

17. Ibid.

18. Ibid.

19. Schaefer Interview.

20. Ibid.

21. Mott, *History*, vol. 5, p. 42.

22. Ibid., p. 43.

23. Ibid.

24. Reuss, "Better Homes," p. 76.

25. Ibid.

26. Meredith Company file, October 1971.

27. Mott, *History*, vol. 5, p. 44.

28. *Annual Report*, Publishers Information Bureau, Inc., 1950-1960.

29. Reuss, *Better Homes*, p. 80.

30. Robert Burnett, president, Meredith Corporation, address delivered to *Better Homes and Gardens* Advertising Sales Conference, Innisbrook Hotel, Innisbrook, Florida, November 10, 1977.

31. Rehm Interview.

32. Ibid.

33. Publishers Information Bureau research records, 1946-1954.

34. Letter from W. F. Jones, former New York advertising director, *BH&G*, January 30, 1978.

35. Ibid.

36. Mott, *History*, vol. 5, p. 45.

37. Ibid.

38. Personal Interview with Hugh Curley, research director, *BH&G*, December 1, 1977.

39. Ibid.

40. *BH&G* News Bureau file, August 1, 1947.

41. Mott, *History*, vol. 5, p. 46.

42. *BH&G* file, October 1956.

43. Ibid.

44. "Your Home Is Where Our Heart Is," *BH&G* (September 1947), p. 27.

45. *BH&G* News Bureau file, August 1, 1947.

46. Rehm Interview.

47. Ibid.

48. Ibid.

49. Statement made at *BH&G* "Five-Oh" Sales Conference, Maui, Hawaii, January 25, 1972.

50. Ibid.

51. Elizabeth M. Fowler, "Inflation Worries Most Consumers But They Lack a Plan to Combat It," *New York Times*, April 8, 1968, p. 73.

52. Ibid.

53. Ibid.

54. "*Better Homes and Gardens* Forms Reader Panel for Product Tests," *Advertising Age* (January 19, 1976), p. 1.

55. Ibid.

56. *BH&G* file, 1971.

57. *BH&G* file, October 1972.

58. *BH&G* 50th anniversary file, October 1972.

59. Ibid.

60. Letter from Kenneth P. Zosel, administrative manager, *BH&G*, Des Moines, Iowa, August 3, 1978.

61. Ibid.

62. Ibid.

63. Rehm Interview.

64. Audit Bureau of Circulations Publishers' Statements, December 1977.

65. Philip H. Dougherty, "Advertising Enthusiast," *New York Times*, July 6, 1970, p. 49.

66. Ibid.

67. "Bailey Leaves Meredith for *LHJ* Ad Post," *Advertising Age* (February 3, 1972), p. 1.

68. Ibid.

69. Ibid.

70. "*Better Homes* Stresses Its Image," *New York Times* (February 6, 1978), p. 90.

71. Ibid.

72. Ibid.

73. "Meredith Borrows $23 Million to Convert *Better Homes*' Format," *Wall Street Journal*, December 31, 1975, p. 1.

74. *BH&G* files, 1975, 1976.

75. "*Better Homes* to Reduce Size of Page in '77," *Advertising Age* (January 5, 1977), p. 1.

76. Personal Interview with Robert A. Burnett, president, Meredith Corporation, New York, New York, August 24, 1978.

77. Ibid.

78. "Meredith and Drake University Team-up for Magazine Seminar," *Imprint* (Spring 1977), pp. 6, 7. A publication of the Meredith Corporation.

79. Ibid.

7

NEWSWEEK

News magazines, or those general magazines devoted almost exclusively to the dissemination of news, became an important part of the magazine industry beginning in 1923. That was the year when Henry Luce and Briton Hadden first published *Time*. For many years prior to the first news magazine, as we know it today, *Review of Reviews*, *World's Work*, *Current History*, and *Literary Digest* dealt with news, summarizing, explaining, and evaluating it.

The news magazines of the twentieth century have been characterized by a distinct journalistic style of presentation. The articles are departmentalized, in a short, lively writing style, winnowing out unnecessary detail, duplication, and repetition. Over the years, illustrations, many in color, have been featured and these magazines, classified today by the magazine industry as newsweeklies, have become profitable business enterprises. Currently, there are three newsweeklies—*Time*, *Newsweek*, and *U.S. News and World Report*.

Analysis in this book is confined largely to the historical development of *Newsweek*, the leader in number of advertising pages for the past 12 years.

FIRST ISSUE OF *NEWS-WEEK*

News-Week was founded by a former foreign news editor of *Time*, Thomas J. C. Martyn. After leaving *Time*, he had worked on the editorial staff of the *New York Times* for six years. Samuel

Thurston Williams, 16 years with the *Times*, and once its Washington correspondent, resigned and joined Martyn as editor of the new publication. The first issue appeared February 17, 1933, with the logotype hyphenated, *News-Week*. It was written and edited in Manhattan at 1270 Sixth Avenue, but was printed at the McCall Corporation plant in Dayton, Ohio.[1]

Martyn held the title of publisher, Edward L. Rea was the first advertising director, and Julian L. Watkins was the first circulation manager. Advertisers were guaranteed an average circulation of 50,000.[2] The first issue featured articles on the farm mortgage problem and " . . . the move to give Franklin D. Roosevelt a 'dictator's powers.'"[3] There followed, in the same issue, articles in departments labeled Sport, Business, Entertainment, and Headliners. The front cover and other pages were devoted to photographs. A year's subscription was $4 and the newsstand price was 10 cents.[4]

In a memo to the staff, Martyn outlined what he believed to be the policy and objectives of the new publication:

> It seems to me to be necessary at this juncture of our growth, for me as publisher, to outline to you, and through you to the editorial staff, the news policy upon which *News-Week* is being directed. Nothing I am about to set down is to be regarded as final, because the experience to which we are all contributing, and which we all are sharing is sure to make changes necessary. Such changes are part and parcel of our profession, and they are wisely made by common direction if each of us recognizes that the stupendous task of getting out a news-magazine once a week is too big a job for any single individual to dominate. Wise changes are progress.
>
> *News-Week* was founded to be a news magazine of newspaper men, by newspaper men for the public. We felt, and I believe quite rightly, that newspaper men are best trained to know the type of weekly service that would most serve the needs and desires of busy citizens. To that end, we dedicated ourselves as explorers and as pioneers, not merely to a new profession, but also to a new art. The common experience we have thus far shared has been a good schooling; it has made our thinking clearer, more practical and, I believe wiser.[5]

Publisher Martyn's financial backing was derived partly from the Cheney Silk family, into which he had married three years previously. Editor Williamson's wife was Cora Marcia Chase, one-time Metropolitan Opera soprano.[6]

Today

On October 28, 1933, a magazine named *Today* was launched, edited by Raymond Moley who, at one time, had been a member of Franklin D. Roosevelt's Brain Trust. Financial assets were provided by Vincent Astor and W. Averell Harriman who hoped to popularize the New Deal. The magazine was widely quoted, but it never went over 75,000 in circulation.[7]

The idea for *Today* originated with Mary Harriman, Averell's sister. She discussed the project with Vincent Astor, and they decided on Raymond Moley as editor. Astor had the largest financial interest in the magazine; the Harrimans' interest was fractional. After his sister's death, Harriman represented her family's interest as well as his own. The magazine was having financial difficulties, and the direction of its operation was discussed from time to time at the board meetings.[8]

Today and *News-Week* Merge

In February 1937, after observing the situation for almost four years, the owners of *Today* decided to merge with *News-Week*. It was planned that the new publication would continue the format and the name of *News-Week* and that it would contain a page of editorial comment in each issue by Raymond Moley. McCall Corporation, which had been printing *Today*, continued to print *News-Week*. Officers of the merged publications were Vincent Astor, president; S. William Childs, Jr., vice-president; F. DuSussoit Duke, vice-president; Raymond Moley, editor; S. T. Williamson, executive editor; and Frank K. White, treasurer.[9]

MALCOLM MUIR

When Malcolm Muir, president of McGraw-Hill, was with the National Recovery Administration, Harriman had become well acquainted with him and had great respect for him. Shortly after Muir left the Roosevelt administration, he had taken over the management of McGraw-Hill, and Harriman learned of some of the techniques Muir had used in developing *Business Week*, a McGraw-Hill publication.[10]

Harriman approached Muir on taking the helm of *News-Week* and induced him to accept the offer. Muir presented a four-year program to Harriman in which he calculated a drop in losses over a period of time, resulting eventually in a break-even status.[11]

Muir assumed management of the magazine on June 21, 1937. His titles were president and publisher, and he was named to the board of directors. He brought with him to his new magazine several executives from McGraw-Hill. Among them were Gordon S. Hargraves as advertising manager, M. W. Perinier as advertising salesman, and Theodore F. Mueller as general manager. He also recruited two advertising salesmen from the *Saturday Evening Post*, John Rutherford and Stanley Whipple. Later, Arthur V. Anderson was named advertising director and W. R. Pelkus, circulation director. On October 4, 1937, the name of the magazine was changed to *Newsweek*.[12]

In accepting the position as head, Muir was taking a risk, having given up a well-remunerated and stable position at McGraw-Hill. However, he believed that his experience at McGraw-Hill was an excellent background for guiding a weekly news magazine. At McGraw-Hill there had been heavy emphasis on accuracy in reporting business news. As president of the organization, he had felt responsible for this accuracy. At *Newsweek* he insisted that the publication become a "Magazine of News Significance," a slogan that later appeared on the masthead. He wanted the facts reported, but he also wanted to have readers understand their significance. He reasoned that interpretive reporting occupied a place in news reporting, but he did not want it mixed with the facts. He wanted reportage of what the story meant, what was behind the headline.[13]

Another newsweekly, *U. S. News*, had appeared on the scene in April 1933, with David Lawrence as editor and publisher. It carried serious national and business news and specialized in official texts and documents. In May 1946, he brought out a sister publication, *World Report*, dealing in foreign news. The two publications were merged into *U. S. News and World Report* in January 1948, since Lawrence had decided it was impossible to tell where international affairs began and national affairs left off.[14]

EARLY ORGANIZATION

Weekly Publications, Inc., was formed as a New York stock corporation by the filing of a Certificate of Incorporation in the office of the Secretary of State of New York on December 23, 1936. On February 20, 1937, Weekly Publications, Inc., acquired all of the publishing assets and publishing business of two predecessor corporations—News-Week, Inc., and Today Associates, Inc. The consideration for these acquisitions was, in the case of News-Week, Inc., assets, $10 in cash, the assumption of certain liabilities, and the obligation of certain contracts. In the case of Today Associates, Inc., the consideration was a similar assumption of liabilities and obligations and the issuance of 100,000 shares of common capital stock of the par value of 10 cents per share and $500,000 principal amount of 5 percent Twenty-year Income Debenture Bonds.[15]

The transaction with News-Week, Inc., was conditioned on commitments from certain interested parties to subscribe $600,000 of cash capital for 120,000 shares of the common capital stock of Weekly Publications, Inc., and $600,000 principal amount of its debentures. The subscribers to the stock and debentures, in varying amounts, were the following: Starling W. Childs, Jr., Richard S. Childs, John Hay Whitney, Lee A. Ault, Alice S. Coffin, Elmer Ericson, and McCall Corporation.[16]

On the side of Today Associates, Inc., the transaction was conditioned on the transfer and assignment to Weekly Publications, Inc., of $250,000 cash, which was to be among the assets acquired from Today Associates, Inc., and the similar assignment and transfer of notes, in the total amount of $250,000, of Vincent Astor and W. Averell Harriman.[17]

Shortly after Muir became the president of the magazine, it departed from its simple digest of the news and announced a three-dimensional editorial formula consisting of the news itself, the background of the news, and interpretations of the significance of the news. In contrast to the pattern at *Time*, *Newsweek* adopted a signed opinion columns policy, beginning with Raymond Moley's column. The writers of the news columns, however, remained anonymous for many years. Also, a crew of editorial researchers was established who aided writers in obtaining information and checking facts for their stories. A news-gathering system of correspondents and bureaus was also set up to supplement the news coverage supplied by the press associations.[18]

THE NEWSPAPER GUILD

The first union agreement was made on January 13, 1939, between Weekly Publications, Inc., and the Newspaper Guild of New York on behalf of all regular editorial employees except bona fide executives. Hours of work were set as well as a minimum wage scale, severance pay, vacations, sick leave, supplies and equipment, no pay cuts, and the establishment of a grievance committee. The duration of the agreement was for a period of one year from the date of signing, January 16, 1939. The signators were: Muir as president, representing the corporation, and the Guild executives, Milton Kaufman, executive secretary, and Ed C. Schneider.[19] Witnesses were John E. Pfeiffer, Gerson Zelman, and Robert G. Whalen. At the time of the writing of this study Zelman was still an employee of the magazine. Writers and staff writers were in the highest pay category with a starting salary of $40 per week, $50 after one year, $65 after two years, and $75 after three years.[20]

A STATEMENT OF CONFIDENCE

There was a period during the Depression when the publication had trouble even meeting the payroll. At times the management had to go to the directors for funds just for that purpose. A particularly difficult year to sell advertising was 1938 and the competition, *Time* to be exact, was suspected of spreading rumors that *Newsweek* was "going down the drain."[21]

When the situation was most desperate, Muir prevailed upon Harriman, Astor, and the several other directors to sign a full-page advertisement attesting to their faith in *Newsweek* and its future. It was published in the *New York Times* and in *Newsweek* in 1938. Copies were also mailed to the entire advertising promotion list. This show of confidence and strength stopped the rumors because it was evident that the directors, who were so well known, would not go back on their word.[22]

The Building of Circulation

The building of circulation, always difficult with a new magazine, was especially so during the Depression for the entire magazine business. *Newsweek* installed a policy of mailing out renewal notices to subscribers whose subscriptions had lapsed. This program was followed up by catalogue agencies, and lastly, field men who actually called on readers in their homes. An attempt was made to build up a reserve of high quality renewals.[23]

The magazine's circulation strength began to be observed by the competition, and Muir recalls a conversation he had early in 1942 with Henry Luce, publisher of *Time*:

Malcolm, it's a strange thing to say, you know I'm glad you took over *Newsweek*. I always felt that damned dirty paper was stepping on my trouser legs behind me. You've gone off on your own and you've given us some pretty good competition.[24]

At that time average weekly circulation was 200,000 and building toward 250,000. By 1939 circulation had reached 330,000. In 1945 an international edition of the magazine was published and printed in Paris, France. During this period the magazine scored one of the industry's noted "scoops," as they are called in journalism, by putting together a detailed victory story which appeared in print even as the bells of liberation were tolling throughout Europe. The man responsible for that coup was Gibson McCabe, who had joined *Newsweek* in 1942 as circulation director, left to join the United States naval forces as a lieutenant, j.g., and then rejoined the magazine toward the end of the war, assuming the position of manager of European Editions in Paris.[25]

WORLD WAR II

During World War II the magazine took advantage of the public's interest in the conflict by starting war news columns and even hiring retired generals and admirals to write for the magazine. One military section was entitled "War Tides," and some of the experts interpreting war news were General Stephen O. Fuqua and Admiral William V. Pratt. When Fuqua stepped down, Major General Paul B. Malone, U.S. Army retired, wrote the column. There was even a British touch when Major General J. F. C. Fuller was hired as a columnist. On April 17, 1944, the magazine began a department called "For Your Information." This was a letter from the publisher, and was patterned after such informal pieces carried by other news magazines.[26]

Starting with 1933 some of the more loyal firms which advertised in the magazine year after year included: Addressograph-Multigraph Company, General Motors Corporation, Remington Rand Corporation, Chrysler Corporation, Ford Motor Company, Schieffelin & Company, National Distillers Products Company, American Telephone and Telegraph, Goodyear Tire and Rubber Company, General Electric Company, Marchant Calculation Machine Company, Cadillac, International Business Machines, and Warner & Swasey Company. All of the above accounts appeared during the first five years of the publication and stayed with the magazine through 1965 and longer.[27]

EXPANSION AND GROWTH

Newsweek continued to grow during and after World War II, even though there was a paper shortage during the war. To combat the latter problem, the production department purchased lightweight paper which enabled them to run more pages of advertising. Newsstand sales were abnormally high, sometimes running into 100 percent of the copies placed for sale. This was very profitable to the company and impressive to advertisers. At the end of 1947 the Pan American edition of *Newsweek* was discontinued, and the international operation in the United States was revamped and curtailed. F. E. Davis was named manager of the international editions in 1948. His staff consisted of his secretary and himself. He made advertising sales calls in the morning, and in the afternoon attempted to administer the editions in Europe and the Pacific. Toward the end of 1948 John Kirby was hired to serve as International Advertising Sales Manager.[28]

Organization Changes

Changes in the organization of the magazine had occurred gradually during the war years and by February 1945, the organization chart read as follows: president and publisher, Muir; managing editor, Chet Shaw; vice-president and general manager, T. F. Mueller; secretary and treasurer, Charles F. Bomer; advertising director, Arthur V. Anderson; director of circulation and manufacturing production, Frank Ware. The board of directors consisted of Mary Cushing Astor, Charles F. Bomer, E. Roland Harriman, who had replaced his brother, Averell, A. H. Lockett, T. F. Mueller, Ronald L. Redmond, and Muir.[29]

Editorial Staff Reorganization

In a staff memo dated July 13, 1956, Muir outlined an editorial expansion and improvement program including the installation of himself as editor-in-chief, a new post, in addition to his duties as president. He moved Mueller up from general manager to publisher and named John Denson as editor. He named his son, Malcolm Muir, Jr., as executive editor and next in command under Denson. He concluded the memo with the statement:

> I would like to add that as a successful enterprise *Newsweek* has reached an all-time high in circulation and advertising volumes. But more important for an institution such as ours, its prestige has

never been higher. This is the kind of foundation we have to build on.[30]

Twenty-fifth Anniversary

In noting the 25th anniversary of *Newsweek*, Raymond Moley, former editor and now a columnist, wrote:

> The *Newsweek* formula broke new ground in the field. The news, national and worldwide, was to be presented fairly, impartially, and with scrupulous accuracy, together with its significance and meaning.
> There were signed columns of opinion. The great tradition of journalism has been public service through the presentation of the news plus leadership through editorial opinion. *Newsweek's* formula was a variation of that: news, plus opinion signed by qualified and responsible contributing editors speaking for themselves.

> My record of continuity at this milepost I offer here with gratitude to a kind Providence and to my associates. The fact that I came from academic life was an advantage, but also a handicap. . . . a great editor said that "the professor is like Sir Malcolm Campbell who drives many leagues to make a measured mile." And so I omitted the windup. Write it, explain it, repeat it and quit.[31]

Production Changes

For the first time, the August 3, 1953 issue of the magazine was printed simultaneously in the East and the West. This gave the editors time in which to handle late-breaking news. The new plant in Los Angeles enabled the publication to make more rapid distribution of the magazines in the fast-growing western area of the country, and at the same time put less strain on the plant in Dayton, Ohio.

About 20 percent of the total press run of well over one million copies was transferred to the West Coast where it was printed in the plant of Pacific Press, Inc., in Los Angeles, California. A new high-speed press costing more than $1 million was installed by the firm to handle *Newsweek's* printing. Copies of the publication printed in this plant were distributed to subscribers and newsstands in the Pacific and Mountain states, as well as in Hawaii, Alaska, and British Columbia.[32]

Corporate Expansion

The name of the corporation was changed to Newsweek, Inc., by the filing of a Certificate of Change in the office of the Secretary of State of New York on April 9, 1958.[33]

On January 12, 1958, two new directors were added to the board, Lewis W. Douglas and Hoyt Ammidon. Both came to the board with distinguished backgrounds and experience. Douglas was formerly an ambassador to the Court of St. James's, chairman of the board of the Mutual Life Insurance Company, chairman of the English Speaking Union of the United States, and president of the Academy of Political Science. Ammidon was a vice-president and trustee of the Vincent Astor Foundation and a former vice-president of the Hanover Bank. The fact that Ammidon was an executive of the Astor Foundation may have had some bearing on later developments concerning the publication's future ownership.[34]

GIBSON McCABE

McCabe was named publisher of the magazine in 1958. Prior to this appointment he had served as advertising manager in 1947, advertising director in 1949, general manager in 1951, and vice-president in 1954.[35]

During the ten-year period from 1950 to 1960 the publication enjoyed a 71.5 percent growth in circulation going from an average of 826,375 to 1,038,679 copies each week. Advertising linage also kept pace with the growth in circulation. In 1960 *Newsweek* published 2,876.90 pages of advertising and ranked in fifth place among all magazines measured by the Publishers Information Bureau, behind the *New Yorker*, *Business Week*, *Life*, and *Time*, in that order.[36] On May 1, 1959, the publishing operation moved to 444 Madison Avenue, in New York City, to the renamed *Newsweek* building. At the time, it was the tallest building on Madison Avenue and located in the heart of New York's advertising and publishing industry. This constituted the third and last move of the company's offices to date. The magazine had started at 1270 Sixth Avenue and had moved in 1941 to 152 West 42nd Street in New York City.[37]

A CHANGE IN OWNERSHIP

Vincent Astor was the principal owner of Newsweek, Inc., from 1937 until his death in February 1959. At that time his 59 percent stock ownership reverted to the Astor Foundation. About 12 percent was owned by Harriman. Smaller blocks of the 300,000 outstanding shares were owned by Muir, now chairman of the board, his family, and some *Newsweek* associates.[38]

Early in 1961, it was rumored that the Astor Foundation was willing to sell its major holding in Newsweek, Inc. There were many parties interested in the purchase, including leading publishers such as Conde Nast, Meredith, and Samuel I. Newhouse. There was even an attempt to form a syndicate of Newsweek employees to buy the firm, but that effort failed. Finally, Benjamin Bradlee, who at that time was Washington bureau chief of Newsweek, approached Philip L. Graham, president of The Washington Post Company, and persuaded him to make an offer for the publication.[39]

As the final negotiations neared, Allan W. Betts, who represented the Astor Foundation interests, in early March 1961, summoned Osborn Elliott, managing editor, and McCabe, president, to his office. Betts mentioned that, among others, they had received identical offers from the Washington Post Company and Doubleday & Company, Inc., and inquired as to which offer these two executives thought they should accept. Both recommended The Washington Post Company, and were told their opinion would carry weight as the foundation wanted the employees to be happy after the sale. Word was sent to Graham at The Washington Post Company, and he arrived in New York on March 9, 1961 to complete the deal.[40]

At the meeting with Luke B. Lockwood and Betts, trustees of the Astor Foundation, Graham wrote a check for $2 million on an American Security & Trust Company checking account to the Vincent Astor Foundation.* He crossed off his own name on the check and signed it The Washington Post Company and underneath Philip L. Graham, president. This was the down payment on a gross total offer of $15 million.[41]

The Washington Post, the principal property of The Washington Post Company, was acquired by Eugene Meyer, the late financier, in 1933 for $800,000, and under his direction it became one of the country's top daily newspapers. At his death, in July 1959, the newspaper had a circulation of 400,000. Graham was married to Meyer's daughter Katharine. Meyer persuaded him to become associate publisher of the newspaper in January 1946, and Graham was named publisher six months later when Meyer became board chairman. Graham became president of the company in 1961.[42]

GRAHAM TAKES CHARGE

Although Newsweek was moving along at a rapid pace, increasing circulation to 1,442,836 and showing advertising linage gains

---

*See copy of cancelled check in Appendix G.

each year, it was evident that Graham had some changes in mind. Soon after making the purchase, he visited the magazine's offices in New York, and assured everyone that his company was going to invest in the magazine and make it an even greater success. He offered to buy any stock owned by employees at more than fair price. McCabe was notified that he would remain as president and be the chief business management executive. Elliott, who was then managing editor under Malcolm Muir, Jr., was named chief editorial executive.[43]

Graham's next move was to bring in Frederick S. Beebe, a lawyer, to be chairman of The Washington Post Company, and chairman of Newsweek, Inc. The elder Muir was moved up to honorary chairman. While these moves were being made, McCabe started a search for a new publisher. After six months of negotiations, L. L. (Pete) Callaway, Jr., was finally hired away from Time Inc., which he had joined in 1937, and had served in executive positions on three of their magazines—Time, Fortune, and Sports Illustrated. He started with Newsweek as publisher in January, 1963.[44]

New Research Project

As often happens in a turn-around period with any business, the magazine underwent strengthened executive responsibility, new editorial leadership, and a new regional advertising formation. A new research study was introduced and entitled "The Audiences of Five Magazines." It was the first time the publication had calculated estimates on total audiences instead of relying on circulation figures as published by the Audit Bureau of Circulations. It was a technique endorsed by the Advertising Research Foundation. Against Time, U. S. News, the Saturday Evening Post, and Life, Newsweek was the most efficient in advertising. The sales department at the publication made excellent use of the study, when making presentations to clients and advertising agencies. Newsweek also instituted seven regional advertising editions which attracted new advertisers. These regions were Eastern, East-Central, West-Central, Southern, Western, California, and Texas.[45]

L. L. Callaway, Jr.

Callaway did not waste any time reorganizing his sales team. His first move was to bring in William Scherman from Life magazine to assume the position of vice-president and promotion manager.

Promotion, research, and marketing serve as back-up and supply sources for the sales staff of a magazine. The new publisher next tackled the sales staff and began a series of moves throughout the country. He changed managers in several offices and brought into the New York sales staff men he considered experts in various advertising fields. He appointed industry managers in liquor, men's fashions, travel, insurance, finance, building products, and automobiles. With The Washington Post Company behind him he was able to pay better salaries and offer better fringe benefits.[46]

It is interesting to observe Callaway's precepts:

> I believe that an advertising space salesman must be basically a student of business. He must know a great deal about his accounts. He should study the annual reports of the company he is assigned; he should follow the news in that company day by day so that, in effect, he is the most knowledgeable man on that company, on his account, of anybody in his business. I firmly believe that this sales staff when it really got rolling became the finest sales staff in the newsweekly field. The record is there for all to see. When I became publisher in 1963, *Time* was ahead of *Newsweek* by 406 advertising pages. In 1968 we passed *Time* in advertising pages.[47]

The records show that from 1968 through 1977 *Newsweek* continued to end each year ahead of *Time* in advertising pages.[48]

GRAHAM'S DEATH

The magazine continued to gain in circulation and advertising revenue. However, the whole company was shocked on August 3, 1963 to learn that Philip L. Graham, the president of The Washington Post Company, who had been ill for about six months, had committed suicide. He and his wife Katharine had been the controlling owners of The Washington Post Company, having been given the voting stock by his father-in-law Eugene Meyer. Shortly thereafter, Katharine Graham declared that she was not going to sell the company, but was going to step in as president and retain ownership in the family. This was welcome news to the management of *Newsweek*.[49]

Changes at the Top

On March 5, 1969, chairman Beebe and president McCabe announced several far-reaching executive changes in business management. Callaway was named vice-chairman of the board and chairman of the executive committee. Succeeding Callaway in the post of publisher and executive vice-president was vice-president and advertising director Harry Thompson. Also named executive vice-president was international editions director Robert D. Campbell, who had been with the magazine since 1949, having started as a member of the San Francisco office's advertising sales staff, progressing to West Coast sales manager, and later New York manager. Circulation director and vice-president S. Arthur Dembner was also elected to the board of directors.[50]

In a joint statement, Beebe and McCabe said:

> Our purpose is to provide an even more vigorous management group that will insure the continued forward momentum of the magazine. In the eight years since *Newsweek* was acquired by The Washington Post Company, the magazine's worldwide circulation has grown by more than one million copies to its current rate base of nearly 2,700,000. In this same period, advertising revenues of the domestic edition have risen from $25,500,000 to almost $53,000,000.[51]

Conditions were stable at the publication for a little more than two years when more top executive changes were announced. This time Katharine Graham and Beebe, president and chairman respectively of the parent company, announced that Elliott, who was editor-in-chief of the magazine, had been appointed to the additional post of president and chief executive officer. He succeeded McCabe, who moved over to vice-chairman of the board and chairman of the finance committee. Callaway thereby moved out of the vice-chairman's post and was named senior adviser.[52]

Elliott had been editor since 1961, and under his leadership many changes were made in the publication's style, content, and format. The magazine's appearance was changed, four-color photography was added, and in the early 1960s new journalistic techniques were developed, combining traditional reporting with public opinion analysis to explore thoroughly the pressing issues of the day, ranging from race relations to poverty, the Vietnam war, and unrest on campuses.[53]

More Executive Changes

It was not long before the executive changes described above gave way to more changes in responsibility. On March 22, 1972, another realignment of high-level executive responsibility was announced by Board Chairman Beebe. He noted that the changes were aimed at continuing the publication's position of leadership—a position it had enjoyed for the past ten years.[54]

Editor-in-chief and president Osborn Elliott was named chairman of the board of Newsweek, Inc., and continued as chief executive officer, responsible for the overall direction of the company; Beebe, who had served as Newsweek's board chairman as well as chairman of The Post Company since 1962, assumed the title of chairman of the executive committee; returned to the post of president, a title he held from 1959 until 1971, was vice-chairman McCabe, designated responsible for the overall supervision of circulation, advertising, production, and other business activities of the magazine;[55] and Campbell, who had been executive vice-president, was named publisher.

Campbell also continued his management responsibility for the International Editions. They remained under the direct supervision of vice-president and managing director Peter Derow, who would figure in subsequent reorganizations. Thompson, who had been serving as publisher, was moved aside into the position of executive vice-president for staff affairs. He left soon thereafter for the presidency of Media Networks, Inc., a related regional advertising sales operation in New York.[56]

One of Campbell's first official acts was to name New York advertising sales manager Jack Mandable, vice-president and advertising director. That post had been vacant since October 1971, when Kerr Collingwood resigned following a heart attack. Collingwood was later named Philadelphia manager.

During the ten-year period from 1968 through 1977, the magazine continued to demonstrate unusual growth in both advertising revenue and circulation. In 1968 the total advertising revenue realized was $52.9 million. In 1977 the gross advertising revenue was $124.1 million. The average weekly circulation in 1968 was 2,287,000, and the circulation revenue was $15.7 million. In 1977 these figures increased to 2,969,000 for circulation and $60 million for revenue.[57]

Beebe's Death

The executives of the magazine were saddened on May 1, 1973 to learn of Beebe's death of cancer at the age of 59.[58] He had served as chairman of the board of Newsweek, Inc. and was very close to the magazine and personally involved in its operations. At one point in his career a Newsweek correspondent was arrested and jailed in

Turkey. Beebe, who was a lawyer by profession, flew there, took matters into his own hands, and was able to secure the man's release.[59]

Post Company President Katharine Graham, who took over as chairman, said:

> In an easy going way, he [Beebe] was very tough minded. He combined a remarkable degree of shyness with that kind of ease that doesn't have to show anything to prove itself. . . . One of Fritz's greatest strengths was his skill and sensitivity as a negotiator. He worked very closely with my husband Phil on the purchase of Newsweek.[60]

Campbell Named President

The publication continued its successful advances in 1973 and 1974, and in May 1975, President McCabe retired early at age 64. Publisher Campbell assumed the additional title of president.[61] In May 1976, Charles Kennedy, who had been serving as publisher of Newsweek International, was named vice-president and advertising sales director, succeeding John Mandable who had suffered a mild heart attack five weeks earlier. Mandable was kept on as director of consumer advertising. Mark Edmiston, who had been circulation director of International, was named publisher, replacing Kennedy.[62]

Elliott Resigns

On October 6, 1976, Elliott, chairman of Newsweek, Inc., decided to resign to become Deputy Mayor of New York for Economic Development. In 1979 Elliot was named dean of the Columbia University Graduate School of Journalism. Campbell was elected chairman and was succeeded as president by Peter Derow, 37 years old. Derow had joined the magazine in 1965 and had worked up through various positions including assistant to the president, vice-president, senior vice-president, and executive vice-president.[63] He left Newsweek to become senior vice-president of CBS, Inc., in September, 1977, and returned to the Newsweek presidency in March of 1978.

For more than a year Campbell retained the title of publisher as well as chairman. In December of 1977, senior vice-president David Auchincloss, who had been with the magazine since 1967, was appointed executive vice-president and publisher at the age of 34. At the same time Charles Kennedy, the vice-president and advertising director, was named a senior vice-president.

More Management Changes

On July 13, 1979, a series of management changes was announced. David Auchincloss relinquished the title of publisher. He retained the title of executive vice-president and assumed new duties under the president. Mark M. Edmiston, who had been president of *Newsweek International* and a vice-president of Newsweek, Inc., was named an executive vice-president with overall responsibility for the commercial operations of the domestic edition. Charles Kennedy was promoted to publisher, and reported to Edmiston. Detroit advertising manager James W. (Bill) Allbaugh succeeded Kennedy as vice-president and advertising director. Howard W. Smith, who had been vice-president of *Newsweek International*, succeeded Edmiston as president of *Newsweek International* and was named a vice-president of Newsweek, Inc.

"All of these moves testify to our management's depth and strength," said president Derow. "With revenues and profits running at all-time highs this year, these moves should help us to assure continued success and distinguished leadership in the eighties."[64]

The magazine continued to lead the newsweekly field in advertising pages during 1977 and 1978, returning high revenues and profits to The Washington Post Company. The marketing department, a support division behind both the editorial and advertising sales departments, was strengthened by the appointment of Arthur E. Karlan as vice-president and marketing director. Karlan was a sales oriented executive who had served as a sales executive and New York sales manager for the magazine for several years following experience in the advertising agency field.

A New Magazine

In October, 1979 Newsweek, Inc., tested a sports magazine entitled, *Inside Sports.* This test was so successful in key markets that the decision was made in December to launch the magazine as a monthly in April of 1980. E. Daniel Capell was named publisher, John A. Walsh editor, and Shepherd Brandfon associate publisher.

Derow Named Chairman

On December 27, 1979, Mark J. Meagher, president of the parent Washington Post Company, announced that Peter Derow, 39, who had been president of Newsweek, Inc., since March 1978, would succeed Campbell, who would retire as chairman on December 31, 1979, after 30 years service with *Newsweek.* It was also announced that Derow would continue to hold the title of president. In announcing Derow's appointment Meagher said, "Peter has played a major role in *Newsweek*'s great strides over more than a decade, culminating in a 1979 performance that has broken all the magazine's records—for advertising pages, revenues, and operating income. He will be a splendid successor to Bob Campbell, with whom he worked closely for many years."[65]

CONCLUSION

Intelligent management and a willingness to reinvest in the product, as profits mounted over the years, certainly contributed to the growth of the publication. In addition to a staff of writers, general editors, senior editors, and executive editors, the magazine in recent years has featured, on a weekly basis, two Nobel Laureates in economics, Dr. Milton Friedman and Dr. Paul Samuelson, and Jane Bryant Quinn, an expert in personal finances. In addition, columnists in the fields of politics, environment, sports, entertainment, and general interest are scheduled regularly.

New production techniques have improved the printing and style of the magazine and enabled it to feature more four-color pages—465 in 1977, four-and-one-half times more than the previous year. Investments were also made in photocomposition procedures, new printing presses, and electronic text copy transmission equipment. The marketing department designated 16 regional and 20 metropolitan editions, available separately or in combination, together with a most successful demographic edition, *Executive Newsweek*, going to 525,000 executives, with personal incomes of $20,000 and up, each year.

Former Chairman Beebe at one time was asked by a college student to describe his philosophy of business management. He wrote the student as follows:

> The best I can do is to say that the most important single ingredient is people. You have to understand and get along with them. You must have some sense of direction that you are trying to move in and to get them to move along with you. Hard work and a questioning mind are also essential. Also a sense of humor and a capacity for enjoying what you are doing would rank high on my list of virtues.[66]

Perhaps the key to *Newsweek*'s success may be found in the quotation above. It is obvious from the above survey of the magazine's business progress that it has been successful. It has become the most profitable division in The Washington Post Company's corporate entity.[67]

Martyn, the founder of *Newsweek*, stated in his first staff memo, mentioned earlier in this chapter, "Wise changes are progress." Over the years the company has not hesitated to make alterations where necessary in both operations and personnel. There have been many changes, but all of them appear to have been in the right direction.

NOTES

1. Personal Interview with Malcolm Muir, former publisher of *Newsweek*, New York, New York, October 27, 1976.

2. Ibid.

3. "A Blank Check for Roosevelt," *News-Week* (February 17, 1933), p. 5.

4. *Newsweek* file, 1933.

5. Memorandum to the editor from T. J. C. Martyn, New York, New York, October 23, 1934, p. 1.

6. Muir Interview.

7. Theodore Peterson, *Magazines in the Twentieth Century*, 2nd ed. (Urbana: University of Illinois Press, 1964), p. 33.

8. Recorded Interview between Averell Harriman and John McAllister, former *Newsweek* general editor, New York, New York, February 5, 1967.

9. "Two Magazine Mergers are Announced," *Wall Street Journal*, February 10, 1937, p. 5.

10. Harriman Interview.

11. Ibid.

12. Muir Interview.

13. Ibid.

14. Peterson, *Magazines*, pp. 333-34.

15. Letter from J. Bay Robinson, partner, Whitman Ransom & Coulson, New York, New York, December 17, 1964.

16. Ibid.

17. Ibid.

18. Peterson, *Magazines*, p. 332.

19. Weekly Publications, Inc., *Newsweek* Contract, with Newspaper Guild of New York, January 16, 1939. See Appendix F.

20. Ibid.

21. Muir Interview.

22. Ibid.

23. Ibid.

24. Ibid.

25. Personal Interview with Gibson McCabe, former president, Newsweek, Inc., New York, New York, January 11, 1977.

26. Calvin Ellsworth Chunn, "History of News Magazines" (Ph.D. diss., University of Missouri, 1950), p. 422.

27. *Newsweek* file, April 1966.

28. Personal Interview with F. E. Davis, senior vice-president, Newsweek, Inc., New York, New York, January 21, 1977.

29. *Newsweek* Masthead, February 12, 1945, p. 2.

30. *Newsweek* Executive Office Memorandum to the staff by Malcolm Muir, July 13, 1956.

31. Raymond Moley, "After 25 Years and Six Days," *Newsweek* (November 3, 1958), p. 112.

32. *Newsweek* file, August 1953.

33. Robinson letter.

34. *Newsweek* file, January 1958.

35. McCabe Interview.

36. *Newsweek* file, January 1961.

37. *Newsweek* files, October 1933; October 1941.

38. Harrison E. Salisbury, "*Washington Post* Buys *Newsweek*," *New York Times*, March 10, 1961, p. 1.

39. Personal Interview with Benjamin Bradlee, former Washington bureau chief, *Newsweek*, Washington, D.C., December 15, 1972.

40. McCabe Interview.

41. Ibid.

42. "Philip Graham Dies; *Newsweek* Publisher," *Herald Tribune*, New York, New York, August 4, 1963, p. 1.

43. McCabe Interview.

44. Ibid.

45. *Newsweek* file, March 1963.

46. Ibid.

47. Personal Interview with L. L. Callaway, Jr., former publisher, *Newsweek*, New York, New York, July 10, 1972.

48. *1978 Fact Book*, The Washington Post Company, p. 12.

49. "Philip L. Graham Dies; Victim of Long Illness Takes Own Life at 48," *Washington Post*, August 4, 1963, p. 1.

50. *N/w.*, (house organ of *Newsweek*), Newsweek, Inc., March 1, 1969, p. 1.

51. Ibid.

52. *N/w.*, Newsweek, Inc., March 25, 1971, p. 1.

53. Ibid.

54. *N/w.*, Newsweek, Inc., March 24, 1972, p. 1.

55. Ibid.

56. Personal Interview with Harry Thompson, former publisher of *Newsweek*, New York, New York, August 3, 1972.

57. *1978 Fact Book*, p. 12.

58. "Frederick Beebe Dies at 59; Chairman of *Washington Post*," *New York Times*, May 2, 1973, p. 48.

59. *N/w.*, Newsweek, Inc., May 4, 1973, p. 1.

60. Ibid.

61. *N/w.*, Newsweek, Inc., May 30, 1975, p. 1.

62. *N/w.*, Newsweek, Inc., May 7, 1976, p. 1.

63. *N/w.*, Newsweek, Inc., October 8, 1976, p. 1.

64. *N/w.*, Newsweek, Inc., July 13, 1979, p. 1.

65. *N/w.*, Newsweek, Inc., December 27, 1979, p. 1.

66. Personal Interview with Frederick Beebe, former chairman, Newsweek, Inc., New York, New York, July 21, 1972.

67. *The Washington Post Company 1975 Annual Report*, The Washington Post Company, Inc., p. 9.

8

LIFE

PICTURE MAGAZINES

Periodicals using illustrations can be traced back to Revolutionary War years. In 1774 Isaiah Thomas published *The Royal American*, which was illustrated by engravings, some even by the famous Paul Revere. New methods of reproduction were devised and, as photography was improved, illustrations became cheaper and more common.[1]

There may be some confusion over picture versus illustrated magazines. Technically they are different. A picture magazine depends on photographs to present its content. *National Geographic*, for instance, is an illustrated magazine; *Life* was and is a picture magazine. The former has considerable text and various photographic illustrations; the latter is dominated by photographs, with text and other types of illustrations secondary. Publishers believed that photographs could convey a message more clearly and dramatically than type.[2]

The pattern for the modern picture magazine was set early by such magazines as *Frank Leslie's Illustrated Newspaper* in 1855 and a year later by *Harper's Weekly*. In the latter half of the nineteenth century, Louis Godey and Sarah Josepha Hale's *Godey's Lady's Book* featured hand-colored plates and black and white drawings.[3]

The *Daily News* and other tabloid newspapers in New York also helped to make photography a tool of journalism. More pictures were used with their sensational, condensed stories than ever before.

Regular newspapers began to use more pictures, a trend aided by the establishment of the Acme Picture Agency in 1923 and the Associated Press Wirephoto Service in 1935. Advertising agencies used cartoons, drawings, and eventually photographs to catch the eye of the reader.[4]

THE FIRST *LIFE* MAGAZINE

John Ames Mitchell, a Harvard graduate in science, had studied architecture in Paris and settled in New York to do illustrating. He decided that this country needed a magazine of pictures, reflecting its life and character. He had a $10,000 legacy in the bank and sought the advice of Henry Holt, a publisher for whom he had been illustrating books. On January 4, 1883, he issued his first publication of a picture magazine and named it *Life*.[5]

This early *Life* was a magazine whose prosperity was securely based on circulation. In 1893 *Life* had made a profit of nearly $100,000, one-third of which came directly from circulation.[6] It was a weekly sold at 10 cents a copy and "bursting" with advertising, in which automobiles and liquors figured prominently. It reached the height of its success just before the United States entered World War I, having weathered the panic of 1907, and kept its circulation at an average of 60,000 each week. Mitchell died in July 1918, and the magazine continued under several owners and editors until the Great Depression, when its advertising linage fell off and it went to a 15-cent monthly in 1932.[7]

As *Time* observed in writing the obituary of *Life*, the magazine ". . . had passed its prime, was definitely on the downgrade."[8] It was not bankrupt, and was making a small profit when, in October 1936, with its November issue on the presses, it decided to give up the battle and accept an offer from Time Inc. The subscription list, features, and goodwill were sold to *Judge*, long its competitor.[9] Its name, which had been purchased for $85,000, was reserved for a new magazine.[10]

On October 7, 1936, George T. Eggleston, editor of *Life*, sent a letter to newspaper and magazine editors as follows:

> Enclosed is an announcement by Clair Maxwell, publisher of *Life*, marking the termination of the fifty-three-year career of the magazine as a humorous publication. Your use of this material will be appreciated.[11]

The news release was headlined, "To All Metropolitan Papers

and All Wire Services," and dated October 7, 1936. The first paragraph read:

> The magazine *Life* was purchased by Time Inc. today and with the November issue will terminate the career of fifty-three years as a humorous publication. This announcement was made by Clair Maxwell, president of Life Magazine, Inc. Mr. Maxwell explained that Time Inc. is completing plans to publish next month a new magazine of the same name but no longer in the field of humor and satire. Henry R. Luce, president of Time Inc., said: "Within two or three weeks I hope to be able to make public our plans for the new *Life*." [12]

TIME INC.

The parent corporation behind the founding of the modern-day *Life* magazine was Time Inc. (officially named without the comma). Briton Hadden and Henry Robinson Luce became friends while sophomores at Yale. After graduation, some army service, and working on daily newspapers, they resigned from their positions on the *Baltimore News* on February 6, 1922, and two days later set out for New York City. They rented office space at 141 East 17th Street and began work on a prospectus that would eventually lead to a gigantic magazine publishing enterprise. [13]

By the end of October 1922, the two men had $86,975 pledged in stock from among their friends and acquaintances and decided to incorporate. Judge Robert L. Luce, another Yale man and distant cousin of Luce, handled the legal formalities, without a fee; the date on the incorporation papers was November 28, 1922. It was 42 weeks since the audacious young entrepreneurs had left Baltimore; now with almost $87,000 of other peoples' money, they were launched. If one had invested $50 in Time Inc. stock in 1936, by the year 1968, this stock would have been worth $74,461. [14]

A Prospectus for a New Magazine

Luce had been thinking about establishing a picture magazine to go along with his now successful *Time* for several years. An experimental department had been established in 1934 for just that purpose. As the organization had done with other projects, experts were acquired who knew photography and its editorial possibilities. In December 1935, the R. R. Donnelley & Sons Company, which printed *Time*, began a series of experiments in printing that would do justice to photographic illustrations by bringing out more detail. The experimental department began serious work on an idea for a picture supplement for *Time*.

A wholly owned subsidiary, Pictures, Inc., was set up to acquire, for the Time Inc. magazines, the rights to pictures from all foreign and domestic agencies. In June 1936, Luce made a formal presentation to the directors. The magazine proposed would be printed on coated paper, better than *Time*'s, but not quite as good as that of the most expensive magazines. It would contain 40 to 48 pages of editorial matter, backed up by 20 pages of advertisements. The price would be 10 cents on the newsstands and $3 per year.[15]

A proposed budget for 500,000 circulation with an advertising rate of $2,000 a page was submitted to the board.[16]

Income

1,000 pages of advertising @ $1,700 net	$1,700,000
500,000 circulation	1,300,000
	$3,000,000

Expenses

Paper and Printing	$2,200,000
Editorial	250,000
Selling Ads	250,000
Circulation Promotion	200,000
General	100,000
	$3,000,000

The entire prospectus of the new publication was outlined in *Tide* magazine, a trade publication. It included the purpose, the need and opportunity, the sources, the forms, and the editorial content. The promotion department referred to the new publication as "The Show-Book of the World."[17]

The Launching of *Life*

The directors approved, and the first issue of the new *Life* was published on November 23, 1936. The cover was a picture of the massive Fort Peck Dam being built in Montana by the Works Progress Administration (WPA). Inside was an aerial view of Fort Knox and a photograph of the new Bay Bridge in San Francisco, as well as other more general scenes and stories. The magazine's page size measured 13-1/2 inches by 21 inches, very large by 1936 standards.[18]

Luce designated himself as managing editor. His alternate, he said, would be John Martin, who would take over when the magazine was successfully underway.[19] The first issue of the publication, containing 96 pages full of photographs, sold out immediately, and customers were requesting newsstand dealers to put their names on waiting lists and were paying as much as $1 for secondhand copies.[20]

Prior to the publication of *Life*, the management was well aware that a strong competitor in the form of another picture magazine was about to be published. It was to be named *Look* and was in the formation stage for ten years. It evolved from the rotogravure section of the *Des Moines Register and Tribune*, which was owned by Gardner Cowles, Jr., and his brother John Cowles.[21] The brothers knew of Time Inc.'s plans and even exchanged ideas to the extent that they offered Luce and his directors a 20 percent interest in their magazine, which amounted to 50,000 shares for $100,000. John Cowles wrote Roy E. Larsen, one of the Time Inc. directors, "Although it is an extreme gamble, we think it is a chance worth taking. . . . Circulation might conceivably go to 600,000 or 800,000 the first year . . ."[22] The Time Inc. executive committee agreed to the investment. At the Cowles' request, it was reduced to 45,000 shares before publication started. In July 1937, with both *Life* and *Look* publishing, the Cowles requested that Time Inc. resell them its interest, which the company did for $157,500, or a profit of $67,500.[23]

LIFE'S EARLY SUCCESS

In 1937 picture magazines had become an American vogue. The success of these publications seemed to bear out the famous slogan of William Randolph Hearst: "A picture is worth 1,000 words."[24] In eight months *Life* spent $167,000 on a library of pictures. Out of 19 pictures purchased, two might be used in *Time* or *Fortune* and the remainder filed in Pictures, Inc. Charter subscribers had been solicited at $3.50 a year, and more than 250,000 persons sent in checks and postal money orders, showing their curiosity about the new magazine. Along with the success in circulation, advertising contracts of $1.7 million at $1,500 a page were sold for the first year, on an average weekly circulation basis of 250,000.[25]

Due to the fact that newsstand sales were so high, distribution became a problem. Dealers were easily selling 450,000 copies each week, and customers were still demanding issues. Dealers complained that the sale was controlled; they only received as many copies of *Life* as they took of *Time*. By the seventh issue, dated January 11, 1937, the print order was for 760,000. Advertising rates for 1937 were doubled to $3,000 for each page. The picture displays had a varying influence on advertisers. It was felt that advertisers would be stimulated to use better art, more pictorial displays, and more and better typographical pages. For instance, the H. J. Heinz Company of Pittsburgh searched through more than 57 pieces of photographic art to produce a pictorial advertisement to complement *Life*'s editorial pictures.[26]

The 38 pages of advertising in the first issue of *Life* represented gross advertising revenue of $64,500. *Life*'s initial circulation guarantee to advertisers was 250,000. However, the first issue sold 466,000 copies, and because of the demand, each subsequent week's print order went beyond the guarantee. Average weekly circulation in 1937 was 1,195,202. When the first issue was published, the United States was still in the midst of the Depression, and the New Deal was in full swing.[27]

In a letter to charter subscribers in July 1937, the publication reported, "*Life* is losing $2,500,000 this year, $50,000 a week, but we are losing it cheerfully. We never expected to make a profit selling a 35-cent magazine for a dime."[28] Treasurer Charles Stillman put it this way, "We did not realize that circulation might go to one million. . . . In the face of demand like that, all our previous plans had to be revised."[29]

In April 1937, Luce appeared before an audience of advertisers and agency heads, and he made an unusual request:

> I stand before you as a court. Here today I make application, not for a few incidental pennies. I ask that you shall appropriate over the next ten critical years no less than 100 million dollars for the publication of a magazine called *Life*. You cannot escape a reply to this question. We will not let you. We will keep hammering persistently on your doors, asking for the money week after week. You will either give it to us or you will not. If you do, there will be *Life*. If you do not, there will be no *Life*.[30]

Two months after this speech, the publication announced a new rate for 1938 of $5,700 for a black and white page of advertising, based on a circulation guarantee of 1.6 million copies each week. This new rate was up 280 percent from the initial space rate of the previous year. By the end of 1938 a new circulation rate base of 2 million was reached and passed, and in 1939, *Life* doubled the advertising revenue and page total of 1938.[31]

The First Magazine Reader Research

Although *Life* was doing splendidly in subscription and newsstand sales, its publisher, Larsen, and others on the executive committee were not satisfied. They strongly believed that their magazine, whether received through the mail or purchased at a newsstand, was passed along to many others, in and out of the household. They thought that audited circulation was not the final measure of what a magazine delivered to advertisers in the way of readership.

In 1938 the magazine evolved the first Continuing Study of Magazine Audiences, utilizing the services and sampling techniques of the Crossley Corporation. The first report indicated average readership for each issue of 17.3 million or 16 percent of the United States population ten years of age and over. These reports were issued annually thereafter.[32]

Few advertisers doubted the wisdom of the adage that advertising effort must be continuous to be effective. A *Printers' Ink* study of ten magazines found that more than 55 percent of the advertisers in eight magazines used three or fewer insertions a year, while more than 20 percent in all ten used one insertion only.[33] During the summer of 1940, Cornelius Dubois, *Life's* research director, undertook to study the effects of continuity in magazine advertising on sales. As a precedent he released a report written in 1916 by Dr. E. V. Strong, Jr., of Stanford University, and published in the *Journal of Experimental Psychology*. It showed that readers forgot 70.5 percent of the advertisements they saw in a month and 83 percent of them in four months.[34]

DuBois hired Samuel E. Gill to test some recent advertising campaigns in a number of cities. This advertising was tested by interviews in New York; Dayton, Ohio; Baltimore, Maryland; and Omaha, Nebraska. To housewives in each city, homogeneous as to age and income, the interviewers showed scrapbooks containing advertisements from the past 12 issues of *Life*, *Saturday Evening Post*, *Time*, and *Look*. Represented were food, drug, and oil products whose copy had appeared at regular intervals.[35]

With these data, *Life* first made some comparisons to show the importance of continuity per se. In practically all cases, the more advertisements a company ran, the more people read its message. For example, 104 people in Omaha saw the first Mobil gas advertisement in a series; the second attracted 50 people who had seen advertisement number one and 43 additional people.[36] Other effects were traced in the study, and it was an example of intelligent research efforts by the magazine that were to continue in the decades ahead.

Merchandising Support

Almost from the first, retailers throughout the country recognized the local impact of this fast-growing publication. In 1941 *Life* set up a merchandising program, and at one point some 200 stores tied in with an editorial story. It was emphasized that the program was to aid retailers to capitalize on nationally advertised products to the fullest extent possible, but that it was not to be rigged or forced. The emphasis was to be on spontaneous dealer enthusiasm. Display materials were sold at cost, not given away.[37]

With World War II, advertising and merchandising plans vanished, just as did many of the products *Life* had been advertising. The situation became so acute that space salesmen, in selling the magazine, also had the task of trying to convince advertisers, because of the shortage of paper, to cut down on their space demands. Despite restrictions, the magazine achieved two significant milestones: it became first in circulation as well as advertising revenue among all magazines, except Sunday supplements. During the years 1942 to 1945 circulation and advertising page totals were held relatively stable.[38]

After the war the company embarked on several projects, among them an effort to allow for the natural growth pattern of the magazine's circulation, interrupted by the war. Even though the newsstand price was increased from 10 cents to 15 cents, in the first postwar year, its average weekly circulation rose from 3.9 million to 4.9 million. An extensive long-range plan was organized with the cooperation of the printers and the suppliers to increase production capacity to make possible expanded circulation. The new program represented an investment of about $50 million, shared by Time Inc. and suppliers.

In 1949 the full effect of the program began to be felt. There was improvement in the production quality of both editorial and advertising pages, closing date requirements were moved up to benefit advertisers, and the magazine was printed at near newspaper speeds, made possible through improvement in ink-drying and press speeds. The publication's advertising revenue surpassed every other magazine, as well as the major broadcast networks. In 1948 the newsstand price had gone up again to 20 cents. Despite this increase, circulation rose to a weekly average of 5,381,942.[39]

The Study of Accumulative Audience

For a period of ten years, *Life* had sponsored and financed the Magazine Audience Group's Continuing Study of Magazine Audiences. It had been a useful research and promotional tool, as these studies measured the magazine's total readership for each average issue. In 1947 these studies were dropped, with no reason given. However, in April 1950, the publication announced a new research project which was revolutionary, monumental, and expensive. It was undertaken by Alfred Politz Research, Inc., and was titled "A Study of the Accumulative Audience of *Life*."[40] It was believed that this study would set new horizons for media investigations and chart the major directions of important magazine research for years to come. Howard Black, executive vice-president and director of advertising and public relations, stated:

> Other magazines, using Politz's methods and criteria to conduct similar studies along the same lines, would contribute greatly to the whole magazine industry.[41]

The significance of this new study lay in the fact that for the first time a publication was in a position to measure its cumulative audience. It would reveal not only how many people read any average issue; it could also tell how many separate people were reached by one or two, 12 or 13, or any number of issues; it could disclose how large a proportion of readers was new for any issue and what proportion of readers had seen the issue or issues before.

Publisher Andrew Heiskell stated:

> For the first time in publishing history, advertisers, agencies, and others interested in media research can see the specific readership accumulation developed by a magazine over a period of weeks or months.[42]

The study enabled *Life* to offer a six-time advertiser evidence of an audience potential of 52.5 million and a 13-time advertiser a potential audience of 62.6 million.

In 1952 the American Institute of Management included Time Inc. in its list of the ten best-managed corporations. This designation was amusing to the executives at the company.[43] They believed that they did not conform to Harvard Business School norms. As explained by Luce, "The one thing which is unusual about Time Inc. is that we have to combine the practice of journalism with *all* aspects of any other business organization."[44]

THE TWENTIETH YEAR

An average issue of the magazine in 1956, with 5.7 million weekly circulation, required 4,000 tons of paper, 100 tons of ink, and filled 90 freight cars. The original battery of eight presses had grown to 30 high-speed units. The printing facilities were not owned by Time Inc., but rather by R. R. Donnelley & Sons in Chicago, the Pacific Press in Los Angeles, and Cuneo Eastern Press in Philadelphia.

There were 22 domestic news bureaus and advertising offices in the United States and 17 outside of the country in 1956. The headquarters of *Life* and Time Inc. were at 9 Rockefeller Plaza in New York, with circulation offices in Chicago. By this time, the corporation was also publishing *Fortune*, *Sports Illustrated*, *House and Home*, and *Architectural Forum*.[45]

After General Douglas MacArthur's return to the United States from Japan, *Life* attempted to persuade him to write his memoirs. He spurned all offers. However, in 1954 his aide and confidant, Major General Courtney Whitney, offered the editors his story of the general. As publisher Heiskell put it, it would be "MacArthur who speaks, even though the by-line is Major Whitney."[46] Excerpts from the book under the title "MacArthur's Rendezvous With History" appeared in the summer of 1955.[47]

The issue of MacArthur's behavior in Korea was revived when *Life* published the second volume of Harry Truman's memoirs. They paid $600,000 for these rights, with right of resale, including book publication and newspaper syndication. Truman was attracted by the offer because Congress had not yet provided a pension for ex-presidents, and he had no substantial private means. It was a good business deal for the magazine. After the resale of the rights, the magazine's out-of-pocket cost for the ten installments, which appeared in the fall of 1955 and in early 1956, was little more than $100,000.[48]

The magazine industry suffered a shock in December 1956, when it was announced by the Crowell-Collier Publishing Company that it was discontinuing the 68-year old *Collier's* and the 83-year old *Woman's Home Companion*. A loss of $7.5 million, which the two magazines suffered that year, threatened the existence of the parent company and its profitable record, book publishing, and encyclopedia operations.[49]

Life's management considered taking over all, or part, of the unfulfilled subscriptions of *Collier's*. The temptation was strong, but the magazine's advertising director, Clay Buckhout, was not certain that increased circulation, derived from *Collier's*, could be sold to advertisers. Circulation director John Hallenbeck was doubtful about the added value of such an investment because *Life* already had a very healthy circulation. The management also did not want to make a move that might disturb a profit pattern. In December 1956, the publication was completing a record year of $17.4 million in net income.[50]

Look's management saw the *Collier's* offer as a golden opportunity. They purchased the lists, offered advertisers a 15 percent increase in their circulation base, with no increase in cost for each thousand circulation, and in 1957 increased advertising revenue by $9 million.[51]

At this time, there was evidence that media battle lines were forming for the sole purpose of attracting readers to their publications and viewers to their network television offerings in order to attract advertising dollars. Four mass magazines of general interest were now competing for the advertising dollar. These four were *Reader's Digest*, which began accepting advertising in 1955, *Life*, the *Saturday Evening Post*, and the biweekly, *Look*. In four years, from 1952 to 1956, advertising expenditures in television had risen from $453,900,000 to $1,206,700,000.[52]

TROUBLE LOOMING ON THE HORIZON

In the spring of 1961, a reporter from *Newsweek* interviewed C. D. Jackson, publisher of *Life*. He asked him about the 130-page loss in advertising for the first three months of the year, about rumors that staffers had been released and that the magazine's production costs were overwhelming the publication's low 19 cents net newsstand price. It was evident in the taped interview that Jackson was becoming irritated over questions about *Life*'s alleged weaknesses. He retorted:

> *Life* will survive very, very profitably. There is a tremendous swing on the part of advertisers towards the printed word and I think *Life* is the cornerstone ... There is a great generalness setting in over our lives ... We had seven million copies of a four-color cover around the country by Wednesday after the inauguration, and hell, there's a price to pay for that ... We invented the concept of pictorial science coverage. Look at this issue. There's no hole in that coverage. Where do you see a flaw? Nowhere ... You're goddamn right we're in good shape, and we're not going to stay that way complacently but competitively. Are we on top of the heap? You're goddamn right again.[53]

Jackson was optimistic about the magazine's advertising picture. "I don't have the figures at hand," he hedged. "But I'm extremely happy about the advertising picture."[54] Pressed further about declining advertising linage he said, "You have the figures."[55] With a smile and his ninth chain-smoked cigarette in an hour burning in the ash tray, Jackson ended the interview.[56]

A Slow-Down in the 1960s

Life's quantitative advantage over the competition was beginning to diminish; newsstand sales continued to decline and advertising sales were slow during the early 1960s. There was evidence of
concern even among the top executives at Time Inc. Look's recent
progress and some of the promotion campaigns launched by this
nearest competitor worried Luce. One of these campaigns was built
around the theme "Look likes people." Luce was shown a Look
memorandum sent to an advertising agency:

> Standing above and apart from man, Life—in spite of efforts at
> informality—remains the lofty pundit, superior, condescending,
> jesting, ponderous with moral instruction for the lesser
> masses ... Life sets forth answers; Look asks questions. Life is
> impersonal. Life likes theories ... Look likes people.[57]

Luce's reaction to the memo was that it was taking a surefire
American line. He said that he felt there was another personal reason
Look thought its "impersonality" charge would be effective. That
personal reason was himself. He said he had been widely regarded as
aloof, cold, and inhuman, and he was sorry for Life's sake.[58]

Top-level Changes

In April 1960, there were important high-level changes in the
corporate structure that affected the magazine. Luce and Larsen
announced that Heiskell would become chairman of the board,
replacing Maurice T. Moore; James Linen would become president,
with Larsen becoming chairman of the new executive committee.
David Brumbaugh was named executive vice-president, treasurer,
and a director. Although problems were in the offing for Life, the
parent corporation was enjoying a period of record revenues. Total
assets were now $230,585,000.[59]

During the period 1960-64 the new management team was able
to report that they had increased revenues from $287,121,000 to
$412,507,000 and net income from $9,303,000 to $26,526,000. These
figures were the result of expanded sales in all divisions and continued control over costs. Beginning in 1950, the corporation, through
the Life division, had published a number of very profitable books.
Late in 1959, Jerome S. Hardy, a vice-president of Doubleday &
Company, joined the publisher's staff to take charge of book projects.
In 1961 a separate division was opened and Hardy was named
publisher of Time-Life Books.[60] By 1964 the division was selling nine

million volumes in the United States and Canada and two million abroad in 11 languages. Also in 1964 the revenues of Time-Life Broadcast were at a new high level.[61]

The Death of Henry R. Luce

Luce, in retirement, continued to write and deliver speeches, pursuing his philosophic inquiry into the law and its potential for world peace. He had experienced a pulmonary embolism while vacationing at his home in Phoenix, Arizona, on February 5, 1958, two months before his 60th birthday. He continued a busy retirement schedule for the next several years. On February 27, 1967, at the age of 68, the world-renowned publisher died of a heart attack. Only the week before, he had been at the corporation headquarters in New York, exuberantly questioning and criticizing staff members.[62] His will stated:

> Time Incorporated is now, and is expected to continue to be, principally a journalistic enterprise, and as such, an enterprise operated in the public interest as well as in the interest of its stockholders. I desire that my executors and my trustees shall be enabled to hold my stock ... and to vote such stock in the best interests of said corporation ... as a journalistic enterprise.[63]

Problems at *Life*

By October 1967, *Life*'s advertising linage was off 175 pages. In March 1964, Hardy had been moved from publisher of the book division to publisher of the magazine. He named John U. Crandell as advertising director, replacing James J. Dunn. The magazine's advertising income was down $14 million in 1967. In September 1967, in an effort to stem the tide, Crandell announced a restructuring of the entire sales force along marketing lines with a new five-group sales staff. The divisions were home and auto, business and personal services, drugs and toiletries, grocery products and beverages, and tobacco and confections. The entire sales operation was divided into package goods and durable goods, with Roy A. Lord in charge of the former and Bryce Blynn, Jr., the latter.[64]

In explaining the new sales organization, Crandell stated:

> The rise in the corporate brand manager system has increased the media decision makers in agency and client. In 1957, for example, there were six people for a salesman to see at General Mills. Today, there are 30 of critical importance, 25 of considerable importance,

and 20 of some importance. It has gone the same way at other companies.

> The average salesman, *Life* has 74 in 12 offices, in New York must call on 192 people. The man on top of the list, with 37 accounts and agencies to deal with, has 450 on his people list. We can't pioneer new accounts, we're just hitting the high spots, the cream.[65]

Crandell announced that at least 12 new salesmen would be hired, and they would seek younger men, with three or four years of brand manager or assistant brand manager experience.[66] In other words, he was going after men in client organizations such as General Mills, Procter & Gamble, General Foods, and others.

In May 1968, *Life* had purchased 500,000 of the *Saturday Evening Post*'s subscriptions in an attempt to aid the ailing magazine and also to move ahead of *Look* in circulation.[67] Audit figures for December 1969 showed that the magazine had reached an unprecedented average total paid circulation, including bulk, of 8,560,647.[68]

Life Under the Knife

The purchase of this circulation proved to be a Pyrrhic victory. It put the magazine's circulation so high that, with the accompanying advertising rate increases, it was pricing itself out of the market. Television was becoming a most formidable competitor both in advertising and editorial. Television, covering the world, began to weaken *Life*'s stronghold on picture journalism. The page rate for four-color advertising had gone to $64,200, or $20,000 more than the cost of a minute of television advertising time. Television had siphoned off many of the package-goods advertising dollars that once went to the magazine.[69]

Years of rumors and bad-mouthing had hurt the sales efforts of the magazine, and the demise of the *Saturday Evening Post* on February 8, 1969 did not help curb any of the comments that *Life* would be next. Printing costs had risen along with postal rates, and the company did not believe that the subscriber should pay more for the magazine at that time. Advertising linage was dropping at the rate of 19.2 percent, because the advertisers available for the magazine's high rates were dwindling.[70]

Executive Changes

In a move to strengthen the magazine's management structure, J. Garry Valk, publisher of *Sports Illustrated* since 1965, was named publisher of *Life*, succeeding Hardy who resigned to join the Dreyfus Corporation as executive vice-president. The corporation announced that Hardy's departure was not connected with the recent decreases in the publication's advertising.[71] In the period from January to October, 1969, pages were down 17 percent, from 2,193 to 1,870 pages. Valk had joined Time Inc. in 1946 as a mail clerk. He moved up through positions on the *Time* sales staff in Cleveland and New York to the post of assistant advertising director. In 1963 he moved over to *Sports Illustrated* and served as general manager for a year before being named publisher. In 1966 he was made a vice-president of Time Inc.[72]

In April 1970, *Look* announced a circulation and advertising rate cut, which had an effect on *Life*'s management. Lee Heffner, who had been named advertising director the previous year, replacing Crandell, wrote a staff memo which leaked out to the press. In it he said:

> Obviously *Look* hopes to survive at *Life*'s expense. Make no mistake about it, this is going to be a tough fight. *Look* is desperate. You will hear shortly what we have to counter *Look*'s claims and our arsenal is formidable indeed . . .[73]

To add to the magazine's troubles at this time, Ohio Governor James A. Rhodes filed suit in District Court in New York against *Life* seeking $6.3 million in libel damages. He disputed an article in the magazine, "The Governor and the Mobster," that was published on May 2, 1969. Louis Nizer, Rhodes' attorney, said, "The suit is an attempt to establish the principle that there is such a thing as a public official not having to run this kind of gamut."[74]

In October 1970, *Life* became the fifth major magazine to announce circulation cuts, amid sharply rising publishing, printing, and postal costs. The others were *Look*, *McCall's*, *Holiday*, and *True*. *Life* cut its U.S. circulation by 1.5 million and folded its unprofitable overseas editions.[75]

It appeared to the magazine industry that the above move was inevitable and less drastic than two other possible moves—cutting the page size or switching from weekly to biweekly, as the *Saturday Evening Post* had done four years before it ceased publication.[76]

In cutting back its circulation, the publication reversed its highly controversial 1968 decision to take over 1.3 million subscribers from the *Post*. Although *Life*'s advertising revenues, at $153 million in 1969, were still the greatest in the world, they had dropped by $10 million in the first eight months of 1970. "Taking on those *Post* subscribers was one of the most disastrous publishing decisions ever made," claimed one editor at Time Inc.[77]

Look and Life—Both in Trouble

By December 1970, reports began to circulate that both *Look* and *Life* were in serious difficulty. It was believed that the onslaught of television and special interest magazines was beginning to be felt by the two principal picture magazines, just as it had been with the defunct *Collier's* before them. Even though expenses had been slashed and circulation trimmed, it was estimated that both magazines would wind up the year losing at least $16 million between them.[78]

Life had changed from the weekly picture newsmagazine it had been since its inception to a concentration on more in-depth news and feature stories. *Look* was content to try and reach the more demanding, better-educated reader. It devoted entire issues to zoning, the challenge of the cities, and other subjects. "TV has supplanted whatever fascination *Life* and *Look* offered with their weekly pictures of important news,"[79] contended one top New York advertising executive. "They have a serious problem knowing what form to take in the 1970s."[80]

It was reported that the two magazines, through their chief executive officers, Heiskell of Time Inc. and Cowles of Cowles Publications, had met to discuss their problems. The talks were supposed to have ranged from combining the two advertising sales staffs to an outright merger. Cowles conceded:

> Heiskell and I are very good friends. We have met on a number of occasions to exchange ideas on advertising and circulation—we have mutual problems, you know. We did have some casual conversations about putting the two magazines together. But it was obvious within three minutes that it wouldn't make any sense.[81]

As circulation costs and advertising rates rose from 1960 on, the same dollars bought fewer pages. Media directors were quoted as saying, "They were just about pricing themselves out of the market."[82] Probably in answer to these criticisms, *Life* cut its four-color page rate from $64,000 to $54,000. To counteract this loss, the magazine raised its subscription price 20 percent, and retained its newsstand price at 50 cents. Publisher Valk stipulated, "When your editorial product goes into many millions of copies, your major costs are printing, paper, and distribution—the three costs that drop with fewer copies."[83] Since 1969 the *Life* staff had been cut from 615 to 475.[84]

The advertising picture at *Life* from 1960 through 1970 indicates how page volume shrunk even though the dollar volume remained stable:

LIFE

Year	Pages	Dollars
1960	3,360	$138,784,242
1961	3,158	138,089,532
1962	3,003	140,585,848
1963	2,956	143,875,277
1964	3,235	158,716,645
1965	3,247	163,208,795
1966	3,300	169,693,756
1967	2,972	155,746,055
1968	2,762	153,921,725
1969	2,392	153,272,371
1970	2,046	132,300,000 [85]

The Demise of Look

At the point when industry leaders believed that both Look and Life would weather the high costs of publishing and the sluggish economy, they were shocked to learn that Look planned to cease publication with the issue of October 19, 1971.[86]

When questioned about the effect on Life of this loss of an archrival, Valk commented:

Well, nobody here is walking around with a long face. But, on the other hand, nobody is toasting the loss of our major competitor. It's not as if we didn't have any competition left. There's still TV to contend with. There's also other magazines such as Reader's Digest and TV Guide.[87]

Life still faced problems and foremost among them was the proposed postal increase which was considered by Cowles' executives as the ". . . straw that broke the camel's back."[88]

Heiskell, when questioned about Look's problems, stated:

It is always bad news for the country when a responsible journal is forced to close down. It is particularly bad news when that development is, in part, engendered by an arm of the government— in this case the postal service . . . If the proposed 142 percent total increase is not drastically reduced, I foresee many other marginal magazines folding, and this will be a serious limitation of the free press of America.[89]

It is not known whether or not he realized how much of a soothsayer he was.

Attempts at Retrenchment

In a further attempt to cut costs and stabilize the economic dilemma, the magazine put through a plan to reduce its circulation from 7 million to 5.5 million beginning with the January 14, 1972 issue. This was in line with the publication's efforts to lower advertising page prices and derive an increased contribution from subscriptions. Valk said, "It is impossible to predict the final outcome of the Postal Service proposals on *Life* magazine. But we know, as structured, they would impose a higher burden on *Life* than other magazines."[90]

One week later, it was announced that the publication planned to eliminate 80 to 90 jobs in an economy move caused by declining advertising revenues and rising costs. The managing editor, Ralph Graves, made the announcement at a noon meeting, adding that 40 or 45 editorial workers would be affected and that 45 jobs would be abolished in circulation, advertising, and other noneditorial fields. This move was on top of the 450 employees laid off by Time Inc. in 1970. At this time, it was estimated that *Life* would end up the year 17.7 percent down in revenue.[91]

The Howard Hughes Fiasco

To add to the magazine's troubles, *Life* (as well as the McGraw-Hill Book Company) was taken in by Clifford Irving, who claimed he had ghost-written an authentic authorized autobiography of Howard Hughes, the billionaire industrialist. *Life* contracted to serialize the book; it was reported that $300,000 had been advanced to Irving. On January 7, 1972, Hughes arranged a news conference (via a $360 phone call) from his retreat in the Bahama Islands to the Sheraton-Universal Hotel in Hollywood, California. He denied ever meeting Clifford and called the book and its proposed serialization a fraud. This charge was promptly denied by both the book publisher and the magazine, a denial they would later regret.[92]

Hughes followed up his phone call by filing suit in Manhattan State Supreme Court to halt publication of the alleged autobiography. Justice Samuel M. Gold issued an order requiring those named in the complaint, which included the publication, McGraw-Hill, and the Dell Publishing Company, to appear in court on January 19, 1972, to show why they should not be enjoined from publishing the Hughes material. In the meantime, *Life* had already advanced its schedule of release dates to February 11, 18, and 25.[93]

THE END OF *LIFE*

As the year 1972 progressed, the business situation did not improve at *Life*. Losses continued in all departments; advertising pages had dropped from a yearly high of 4,655 in 1955 to 1,993 in 1971.[94] Rumors were circulating in the industry, and the trade press and gossip sheets were urging James Shepley, president of Time Inc., to close the magazine. It was evident that the top management of the corporation was striving to keep the publication afloat and, at the same time, attempting to explain their actions to wary stockholders.

Although there had been rumors and staff members had witnessed the recent deaths of *Collier's*, the *New York Herald Tribune*, *This Week Magazine*, and *Look*, the end of the magazine came with "sickening suddenness" to most of the personnel. The announcement came on December 8, 1972, that the December 29th, year-end issue would be the magazine's last. The directors and executive committee of the corporation had made the decision the night before.[95]

It was disclosed that the magazine had lost more than $30 million, before taxes, during the last four years. At the press conference held on the executive floor of the Time-Life Building, Hedley Donovan, editor-in-chief of all Time Inc. publications, said, "This is a very sad day for Time Inc."[96] He added that the company's projections for the next two years showed the possibility of another $30 million in losses. By one account a group of key advertisers indicated that they would not renew their contracts in 1973. Also the publication faced a crippling 170 percent increase in postal rates over the next five years.[97]

Chairman Heiskell said:

> I have often thought that Henry Luce, in addition to being a genius for the 67 years and I don't know how many days of his life, was a genius in choosing the date of his death, because an awful lot of things have happened since [that] he would not have liked. And surely he would have shed a very big tear on this occasion.[98]

On the cover of the last issue of the weekly, a compendium of pictures of the year's events, layout artists inserted their own salute at the extreme bottom right corner, "GOODBYE."[99]

CONCLUSION

It was with extreme regret that the management killed the glamor magazine of the Luce publishing empire. It was claimed in audience research studies that it was read by one of every five American men, women, and children. Unlike Gardner Cowles, who blamed *Look*'s death on postal increases, Donovan and Heiskell carefully avoided naming one primary culprit. Donovan pointed out that it was due to a combination of four or five factors specifically, including fourth-quarter advertising revenue and projections into 1973 and 1974, as well as falloff in circulation renewals at rates higher than the two years past. "We preserved as long as we could see any reasonable prospect of profit," [100] said Donovan. "We can no longer see such a prospect. . . . It could be a burden on our other magazines and the long-term growth and health of the company." [101]

At the final press conference Heiskell told the staffers, "I share with your emotional agony in this decision." [102] He also spoke of the weekly publication's accomplishments—the black and white photo essays, which developed into a new art form, coverage of wars from the Spanish Civil to Vietnam, to the religion series, which became the backbone of the book division. He concluded by saying, "We could be proud of what we did for bringing art and science to the American public in a popular but not unsophisticated manner." [103]

In an interview, Heiskell verified data used in this research. It is correct as reported that he and Gardner Cowles met to discuss a merger of *Life* and *Look* in 1970, and both agreed it would not make sense. Heiskell was also correctly quoted in the *Newsweek* interview in 1972. He attributed *Life*'s failure to the fact that they were publishing a magazine of costly mass circulation, and prices were overtaking the publication. During the last months of publication the management was asked why they did not plan to publish a different type magazine to take *Life*'s place. His reply was that audiences of publications cannot be shifted. [104]

The $30-million loss incurred over a period of four years was staggering, but could have been absorbed. They lost that much publishing *Sports Illustrated*, and still forged ahead. It was *Life*'s loss projected over the next four years that was the final discouraging factor. In commenting on the absorption of the *Saturday Evening Post*'s circulation, he said that this circulation did not renew well, and was, therefore, a burden. [105]

Thus, the 36-year old magazine came to a sad end. *Life* pioneered photojournalism, but it was defeated by television. Time Inc. executives tried every conceivable adjustment to bring the publication out of its doldrums without success. It was apparent that the trend was destined to continue downward in spite of changes in top personnel, the cutting of rates, and the reduction of circulation. There are situations where a management has to demonstrate as much courage in closing down an operation as in forcing it to continue. This was one of those occasions, and it was faced with fortitude.

Life **Magazine Born Anew**

On April 24, 1978, editor-in-chief Hedley Donovan and chairman Andrew Heiskell announced that Time Inc. would begin publishing a new, monthly *Life* magazine in October 1978. In a statement they commented that the magazine field was generally vigorous and it seemed an appropriate moment to bring back one of the great forces in American journalism.[106]

The first six issues of the magazine sold not less than 1,200,000 each issue, although the initial guarantee was set at only 700,000. This unusual development appears to insure the continued success of the publication.

NOTES

1. Roland E. Wolseley, *Understanding Magazines*, 2nd ed. (Ames: The Iowa State University Press, 1969), p. 284.

2. Ibid.

3. James Playsted Wood, *Magazines in the United States*, 2nd ed. (New York: The Ronald Press Company, 1956), p. 360.

4. Theodore B. Peterson, Jr., "Consumer Magazines in the United States" (Ph.D. diss., University of Illinois, 1955), p. 392.

5. Frank L. Mott, *A History of American Magazines*, 5 vols. (Cambridge: Harvard University Press, 1957), vol. 4, pp. 556, 557.

6. Ibid., p. 565.

7. Ibid.

8. "Life," *Time* (October 19, 1936), p. 62.

9. Mott, *History*, vol. 4, p. 568.

10. Wolseley, *Understanding*, p. 285.

11. Letter from George T. Eggleston, editor, *Life*, New York, New York, October 7, 1936. See Appendix H.

12. News release, Life Magazine Inc., October 7, 1936.

13. Robert T. Elson, *Time Inc.* (New York: Atheneum, 1968), pp. 3, 4, 6.

14. Ibid., p. 14.

15. Ibid., pp. 272, 275.

16. Ibid., p. 276.

17. "A Prospectus for a New Magazine," *Tide* (September, 1936) pp. 3-8.

18. Dora Jane Hamblin, *That Was the Life* (New York: W. W. Norton & Company, Inc., 1977), p. 18.

19. Elson, *Time*, p. 287.

20. Theodore Peterson, *Magazines in the Twentieth Century*, 2nd ed. (Urbana: University of Illinois Press, 1964), p. 345.

21. Ibid., p. 351.

22. Elson, *Time*, p. 292.

23. Ibid., pp. 292-93.

24. "The Current Fad for Picture Magazines," *The Literary Digest* (January 30, 1937), p. 19.

25. Ibid.

26. Ibid., p. 21.

27. *Life* file, 1937.

28. Time Inc., *Annual Report*, 1937, p. 4.

29. Ibid.

30. Henry R. Luce, president, Time Inc., address delivered to the American Association of Advertising Agencies, The Greenbrier Hotel, White Sulphur Springs, West Virginia, April 15, 1937.

31. *Life* file, 1939.

32. Ibid., 1938.

33. "Continuity Study," *Tide* (November 1, 1940), p. 13.

34. Ibid.

35. Ibid.

36. Ibid.

37. *Life* file, 1941.

38. Ibid., 1942-45.

39. Ibid., 1946-49.

40. "How Big is *Life*?" *Tide* (April 28, 1950), p. 76.

41. Ibid.

42. Ibid.

43. Elson, *Time*, p. 334.

44. Ibid. Emphasis in the original.

45. *Life* file, 1956.

46. Elson, *Time*, p. 297.

47. Ibid., p. 298.

48. Ibid.

49. Ibid., p. 403.

50. Ibid., p. 404.

51. Ibid.

52. Ibid.

53. Recorded Interview between C. D. Jackson, publisher of *Life*, and Bruce Lee, *Newsweek* reporter, New York, New York, April 11, 1961. Copy in *Newsweek* file.

54. Ibid.

55. Ibid.

56. Ibid.

57. Elson, *Time*, p. 426.

58. Ibid., p. 427.

59. *Life* file, 1960.

60. *Life* file, 1960-64.

61. Ibid.

62. "Henry Luce, 68, Dies in Phoenix," *New York Times*, March 1, 1967, p. 1.

63. Elson, *Time*, p. 483.

64. Philip H. Dougherty, "Advertising: *Life* Mobilizes Sales Battalion," *New York Times*, September 21, 1967, p. 77.

65. Ibid.

66. Ibid.

67. "New Bundle of Hope for Ailing *Post*," *Business Week* (May 25, 1968), p. 42.

68. *Life*, Magazine Publisher's Statement, Audit Bureau of Circulations, for six months ending December 31, 1969.

69. Personal Interview with Jerome S. Hardy, former publisher of *Life*, New York, New York, October 25, 1978.

70. Ibid.

71. "Valk Becomes *Life* Publisher," *Advertising Age* (December 15, 1969), p. 1.

72. Ibid.

73. Philip H. Dougherty, "Advertising: *Life* Salesmen Get Pep Talk," *New York Times*, April 30, 1970, p. 70.

74. Craig R. Whitney, "Rhodes Files Suit Against *Life*, Seeking $6.3 Million for Libel," *New York Times*, April 17, 1970, p. 16.

75. Kent MacDougall, "Time Inc.'s *Life* Magazine Says It Will Cut Circulation 1.5 Million," *Wall Street Journal*, October 2, 1970, p. 49.

76. "*Life* Cuts Back," *Newsweek* (October 12, 1970), p. 130.

77. Ibid.

78. Robert E. Dallow and John F. Lawrence, "Real-*Life* (& *Look*) Melodrama," *Washington Post*, December 29, 1970, pp. C1-C2.

79. Ibid.

80. Ibid.

81. Ibid.

82. "What's Ahead for *Life* and *Look*?" *Media Decisions* (February, 1971), p. 40.

83. Ibid., p. 43.

84. Ibid., p. 44.

85. Publishers Information Bureau, 1971.

86. "*Look* to Fold," *Advertising Age* (September 20, 1971).

87. "*Life* Regrets Demise of *Look*, but Eyes Ad Dollars," *Advertising Age* (September 27, 1971), p. 1.

88. Ibid.

89. Ibid.

90. "Life Plans Circulation Cut," *Washington Post*, November 25, 1971, p. 17.

91. "*Life* Magazine is Eliminating 80 to 90 Jobs," *New York Times*, December 2, 1971, p. 43.

92. Gladwin Hill, "Howard Hughes Tells of His Life in a 3,000-Mile Phone Interview," *New York Times*, January 10, 1972, p. 1.

93. Douglas Robinson, "Hughes Files Suit Here to Block Publication of 'Autobiography,'" *New York Times*, January 14, 1972, p. 30.

94. *Life* file, 1971.

95. Hamblin, *That Was*, p. 304.

96. "The Lingering Death of *Life*," *Newsweek* (December 18, 1972), p. 109.

97. Ibid.

98. Ibid.

99. "*Life*, The Year in Pictures 1972," *Life* (December 29, 1972), cover.

100. "The Lingering Death of *Life*," pp. 109-10.

101. Ibid.

102. Ibid.

103. Ibid.

104. Personal Interview with Andrew Heiskell, chairman, Time Inc., New York, New York, November 21, 1978.

105. Ibid.

106. Time Inc. news release, April 24, 1978, contact, Donald M. Wilson.

9

THIS WEEK MAGAZINE

SUNDAY SUPPLEMENTS

The magazine examined in this chapter is from the grouping, "Sunday Supplements." These magazines have physical aspects similar to the publications previously discussed, but differ in one important manner. They are not sold separately, whether at the newsstands, or by subscription. All Sunday supplement magazines are distributed by newspapers, as part of their Sunday editions in individual metropolitan areas. They are printed outside of the host newspaper plant and shipped to the particular newspaper in time for Sunday distribution.

Syndicated national Sunday magazines first appeared in 1869, when a supplementary section was added to the San Francisco *Sunday Chronicle*. By the early 1880s other metropolitan newspapers were featuring such sections in their Sunday editions. When William Randolph Hearst entered the New York journalism scene in 1895, he hired Morrill Goddard, a Dartmouth graduate who had been a reporter for Joseph Pulitzer's New York *World*. Hearst instructed Goddard to create a Sunday magazine for his New York *Sunday Journal*.[1]

American Weekly

Thus on November 15, 1896, the *American Weekly* was born. It was later included in Hearst's San Francisco *Examiner* and subsequently in other Hearst newspapers as they were added to the chain. This was the first nationally syndicated Sunday magazine, and it became a most successful and prosperous publication. This original idea was copied not only by syndicated national Sunday magazines, but also by locally published and edited supplements.[2]

The *American Weekly* was followed by *This Week Magazine*, *Parade*, and *Family Weekly*, constituting the four nationally syndicated Sunday magazines. A detailed analysis of *This Week* follows, since it became the leader in both circulation and advertising volume over a 20-year period starting in 1950.[3]

Euclid M. Covington

The idea for *This Week* originated with Euclid M. Covington in the late 1920s, when he was eastern advertising manager of the Chicago *Herald Examiner*. He believed the successful, well-known metropolitan newspapers of this country would appreciate and be willing to help support a fine family magazine—in contrast to the sensational, gossipy *American Weekly*, distributed solely by Hearst newspapers.[4]

Covington conceived a true Sunday newspaper magazine, one that would carry the best fiction and features; be printed on a superior grade of newsprint; and be the size of such magazines as *Collier's* and the *Saturday Evening Post*, rather than the full newspaper size of the *Weekly*.[5] He resigned from the *Herald Examiner* in 1930 and moved to New York. With very little capital, he decided to put his idea into dummy form for presentation to prospective newspaper publishers. It was printed in four colors and, as seen by the author, was very similar in style to the magazine that was later published.[6]

In 1931 Covington set out, at his own expense, to contact the better metropolitan newspapers from coast to coast. He carried with him the dummy of the prospective magazine, a written presentation of his Sunday magazine idea, and a conditional contract, providing that, if a sufficient number of newspapers had not signed up by a certain date, the contract would lapse.[7]

At the beginning of the Great Depression, the very friendly reception his idea received was astonishing. He was unknown, had no wealthy backer, but nevertheless publishers listened. By the summer of 1932 he had interested seven newspapers. With banks closing and the Depression encroaching with increased velocity, he decided to return to New York and wait things out.

Joseph Palmer Knapp

In the fall of 1932 Covington met Raymond Gilleaudeau through a mutual friend. Gilleaudeau was an attorney and also an executive on the staff of Joseph Palmer Knapp, an industrialist and a member of the board of the Metropolitan Life Insurance Company. Knapp also owned the American Lithographic Company, which he had inherited from his father. In 1902 Knapp induced 13 independent metropolitan newspapers to band together and issue their own magazines as the *Associated Sunday Magazines*. Each published a similar 20-page supplement magazine, a little less than tabloid size.[8]

These syndicated Sunday magazines were printed by the American Lithographic Corporation, and by 1906 the total circulation of this syndicated group was slightly over a million a week. By 1914 it was up to 1,411,000, and by 1915 had reached 1,532,000. However, in 1916 the member newspapers began to cancel their contracts for many reasons, including the paper shortage, production costs, critical transportation difficulties, and advertising uncertainties. In 1918 the enterprise ended.[9]

In spite of the failure of his first venture in newspaper magazine publishing, Knapp never lost interest in publishing, as evidenced by his purchase, soon afterward, of the Crowell Collier Corporation. He was also interested in rotogravure printing. When he sold the American Lithographic Company in 1929, just before the stock market crash, the Alco-Gravure division, started in 1910, was retained. Knapp was also instrumental in the development of the patented Weiss Speed-Dry process which permitted colorgravure printing, of magazine quality, at newspaper printing speeds.[10]

Considering Knapp's experience with a Sunday magazine, and his interest in gravure printing, Gilleaudeau agreed to contact Knapp with Covington's new idea. The presentation and dummy went to Knapp at his fishing lodge in the Catskills. Word came back that he was interested. There were many conferences, and discussions carried over to the spring of 1933. President Franklin D. Roosevelt had instituted many of his reform acts, and the economy seemed to be on the upgrade. On the strength of this, the Knapp organization went into action. Gilleaudeau and Covington were assigned the task of going back to the publishers who had previously indicated an interest, and seeking out new ones who fit the planned pattern.[11]

Gilleaudeau was surprised to find, in his travels, that the groundwork laid by Covington was very beneficial. The publishers were not only still enthusiastic about the idea of a rotogravure Sunday magazine of superior editorial quality, but also offered aid in enlisting the support of their fellows. Harry Grant, the publisher of the *Milwaukee Journal*, was the first to sign. Other enthusiastic early signers were Frank Noyes of the *Washington Star*, Frank Morrison of the *Pittsburgh Press*, William Chandler of *Scripps-Howard*, and William Schmick of the *Baltimore Sun*. The support of these respected publishers was an important factor in bringing others into the group.[12]

TWO CORPORATIONS FORMED

Early in 1934 Knapp registered two corporations: Publication Corporation, which was to act as a holding company, and United Newspapers Magazine Corporation, which was the corporate name for *This Week*. Publication Corporation was the parent entity for both Alco-Gravure and United Newspapers Magazine Corporation. Knapp became chairman of both corporations, and he appointed Gilleaudeau president; Clarence Stouch, vice-president and treasurer; and William Daniel, secretary.[13]

THE MAGAZINE COMPANY/NEWSPAPER CONTRACT

A number of different *This Week* contracts were written before the final one was decided upon. Differences of opinion arose on the terms and the interpretation of the legal language. The objective of the terms was to lift the enterprise above the status of a syndicated service, and create the base for a partnership effort, without any of the liabilities of a partnership.[14]

The first printed contract called for the following division of the net advertising revenue: of the total revenue, 15 percent was to be assigned to the sales and administration fund; of the remainder, 10 percent was to go to the editorial fund. If the cost should exceed the 15 percent and 10 percent, the money was to be furnished by the Magazine Company and the deficit accumulated as recoverable in the advances account. After the 15 percent and 10 percent, 90 percent of the remainder was to be divided among the newspapers and 10 percent was to go to the Magazine Company. A modification, inserted later on November 12, 1934, specified that if the advertising pages averaged fewer than four for each issue a month, Alco-Gravure, Inc., would reduce charges by 10 cents a column for each thousand circulation but not in excess of $1 a thousand.[15]

The first meeting of the newspaper publishers and the magazine company was held September 20, 1934, in the Waldorf-Astoria Hotel, New York City. Fourteen newspapers were represented at the meeting presided over by Knapp. After discussion on memoranda and suggested contract changes, an important second modification was added. It was decided that a general conference board of seven-member newspaper publishers should be substituted for the editorial board, mentioned in the first contract, and the following newspapers were designated to be represented on this board: New York Herald Tribune, the Baltimore Sun, the Boston Herald, the Milwaukee Journal, the Cleveland Plain Dealer, the Chicago Daily News, and the Dallas News. The newspaper publisher representatives were elected to serve until the next annual meeting.[16]

It took 18 months of gestation to arrive at a contract that was mutually acceptable, to agree on an editorial formula, and to bring together the signed contracts of the individual newspapers. February 24, 1935, was the designated starting date. Mrs. William Brown Maloney, who had been editor of the New York Herald Tribune's own magazine section was appointed editor by agreement. At one time she had been editor of the successful women's magazine, The Delineator. It was said that one of her favorite injunctions to her staff was: "Never stop learning . . . Never stop growing."[17] In addition to Gilleaudeau as president, Evans H. H. Hessey was appointed advertising sales director, Thomas Cathcart promotion director, and Covington eastern advertising manager.

THE CONFERENCE BOARD'S AUTHORITY

In drawing up the initial contract, it was decided that the conference board would have three principal jurisdictions: the approval of the designated editor, approval of the advertising rate structure, and approval of newly added member newspapers. It also planned to meet with the top executives of the magazine, on a regular basis, in order to offer advice and counsel.[18]

Under the contract, the member newspapers were to pay production and paper costs for each thousand newspapers circulated. They would then participate in a share of the advertising revenues, again, for each thousand circulated. This revenue share was paid to the newspapers on a monthly basis and profits at the end of the year were divided up by size of newspaper, after the magazine company had taken out its administrative, sales, and editorial costs.[19]

Early in 1935, 21 newspapers had signed contracts, the first being the *Milwaukee Journal* and the twenty-first, the *Boston Herald*.* The first issue of the magazine appeared on February 24, 1935, and contained only 16 pages. The newspaper publishers had opted for first-run fiction as their preference in the new publication. This issue contained the first installment of a serial by Sinclair Lewis, followed by contributions from Fannie Hurst, I. A. R. Wylie, Rupert Hughes, Roy Chapman Andrews, Dorothy Sayers, Neysa McMein, and Ed Wynn. A four-color Beechnut Chewing Gum advertisement appeared on the back cover. The circulation of this first issue was 4,261,000, making it the leader in circulation among all magazines.[20]

MEMBER NEWSPAPER UNREST

It did not take the newspapers long to become dissatisfied with *This Week*. During the first year advertising revenue did not reach expectations, and the editors of the member newspapers were unhappy with the editorial content. Nearly half of the new members sent in protective cancellation notices, effective one year hence as provided in the contract. It looked very discouraging, and Knapp decided something drastic had to be done.

John C. Sterling

Knapp conducted a search of the publishing industry to find an executive whose capabilities and prestige would command respect and confidence. He persuaded John C. Sterling, who was then vice-president and advertising director of *McCall's* magazine, to join Publication Corporation as chairman of the board of directors, and at the same time publisher of *This Week*. *Advertising Age*, a leading industry trade publication, described him as one of the most brilliant and popular magazine executives in the country.[21] Prior to *McCall's*, where he had served ten years, he had been with International Silver Company; Warner Brothers Company; Curtis Publishing Company; and Batten, Barton, Durstine & Osborn, an advertising agency.

The publicity connected with Sterling's new position was helpful, even before he joined the organization. It gave advertisers added confidence in this new venture, since he had left a secure, top position at one of the most successful publishing enterprises. Although his experience had been in the advertising and magazine

---

*List of charter member newspapers in Appendix I.

publishing fields, he had little knowledge of the newspaper business.[22]

His first important task was to visit all of the recalcitrant newspapers. He was on the trip for weeks, calling on the executive staff of each newspaper, all of whom he was meeting for the first time. He attempted to convince them to rescind their cancellations and give the magazine a chance.

He was an impressive man, and told the newspaper executives of new plans for the magazine, the advertising successes, and the plan to appoint a managing editor to aid Mrs. Maloney. In all cases he was successful. The 11 newspapers rescinded their cancellations, and the magazine was able to get back to "business as usual."[23]

First Contract Revision

After Sterling's newspaper visits, the first contract revision was put into effect January 1, 1937. These modifications included a clause on wire stitching, or stapling, which added a charge of 20 cents for each thousand circulation for all issues exceeding six pages of advertising. The staples were important because they gave the magazine a better appearance. No other Sunday magazine at the time had them. There were other modifications involving color printing, and a stipulation that, if there was a deficit in any one year, the magazine company would absorb it. If there was a profit, the proceeds were to be transferred to the general fund.[24]

The first annual meeting, under the revised contract, was held April 20, 1937, in the Waldorf-Astoria Hotel in New York City. Representing the magazine corporation were Knapp, Gilleaudeau, Sterling, and Cathcart. Twenty-two newspapers were represented. William Schmick, publisher of the *Baltimore Sun*, was elected the first chairman and he presided, after the delegates were welcomed by Knapp. The board was enlarged by two places upon motion by Knapp. It was also announced that three newspapers, namely, the *Los Angeles Times*, the *Spokane Spokesman-Review*, and the *Portland Journal*, had joined the original 21. Sterling recommended that an advertising rate increase of 8.3 percent be put in effect January 1, 1938, because of the recent increase in circulation of 10 percent. This was approved.[25]

THE EARLY YEARS

The magazine ended the year 1935 with a total advertising revenue of $1,123,395. This was the highest first-year advertising revenue of any magazine in history. In 1936 revenue had increased to $2,151,199 and in 1937 reached $3,378,908. In spite of these revenue increases, the newspapers were not realizing a profit due to the high weekly purchase cost of the magazine. The first year they lost $696,022, in 1936 $596,110, but in 1937 the loss was reduced to $417,608.[26]

In spite of these losses, the newspapers remained optimistic, and even promoted the magazine within the pages of their own publications. For instance, in 1936 the member newspapers used 271 pages of advertising to promote This Week to their readers.

A spot check was made in ten cities where This Week was available, and it was learned that less than 30 percent of the copies of the publication had been discarded by Tuesday morning following the Sunday delivery date. The advertising department promoted this fact as an indication of the length of life of each edition.[27]

William I. Nichols

In 1939 the management realized that the editorial content of fiction and, in some ways, old-fashioned themes, was not meeting the approval of the newspaper editorial board. William I. Nichols, who had been editor of Sunset Magazine, was brought in as managing editor to assist Mrs. Maloney in producing a more lively magazine. Cathcart was placed in charge of newspaper relations, which meant calling on the present list of newspapers and attempting to induce others to join the group.[28]

From 1939 on, advertising revenue continued to increase, and the average weekly circulation advanced to 5,928,376 in 1942. This Week was now in eighth place among all magazines in advertising revenue.[29] With the advent of World War II, the magazine's progress came to a standstill. Sterling described the situation as follows:

> Unlike many other publications, the war and paper rationing greatly retarded This Week's progress. It had no paper quota of its own, but was forced to depend on the goodwill of each individual newspaper, in order to participate in the ration of each one.
>
> During the war each department of the newspaper was clamoring for more paper. The circulation department . . . the advertising department . . . the editorial department needed a bigger news hole.
>
> There could be no greater evidence as to the publisher's belief in the future of This Week than the fact that all individually gave This Week more than its indicated percentage of their quota.[30]

A New Editor

With the approval of the conference board, Nichols was appointed editor in June 1943. Mrs. Maloney's health was failing, and she was given a three-month leave of absence. Her title was changed to editorial director, placing her in a consultant's role and no longer in charge of the editorial product. While still managing editor, Nichols attempted to put the essence of the magazine's character into a speech.

> In every story we select, we are constantly reminded that *This Week* goes out as part of the local newspaper.... We are reminded of the local editors.... They are our advertisers and friends, telling us constantly what people are thinking throughout the country. Beyond that they remind us that, instead of being sent out from New York by mail, our newspapers are carried down thousands of main streets in an express wagon or on the rack of a bicycle by the local newspaper boy.... All of which means that *This Week* has the priceless opportunity of coming to its readers as a neighbor and friend from down the street, rather than as a stranger from out of town.[31]

GROWTH AFTER WORLD WAR II

There was evidence in 1947 that relations with the member newspapers were not always going to be completely amicable. At a June meeting of the conference board, Chairman Schmick appeared to voice their sentiment when he said:

> I am going to ask some questions about the contract today... nothing is in the nature of criticism. I want to see if we, as a Conference Board, can be constructive.
>
> Now, as I see this contract ... I don't believe there is a chance of the newspapers making any money.
>
> You have a concern known as the United Newspapers Magazine Company.... That company was formed to run *This Week*, and the papers have a management contract with them. Is that right? [Gilleaudeau replied:] In effect, yes. [Schmick:] Who controls *This Week*? Is that controlled by the newspapers or by the magazine company? [Gilleaudeau replied:] I think it is copyrighted by the magazine company. [Schmick:] Then the ownership is in the magazine company ... That leaves the newspapers ... with very little to get hold of. What we own I don't know. We have gone

ahead. . . . Mr. Knapp told us about 48- and 84-page papers, and $8 and $10 a thousand to the newspapers. We have built up a $20-million-dollar business, with the newspapers still losing money, and I see no way of catching up unless we have some kind of a different contract than we have now.[32]

As a result of this verbal outburst, an operating committee of the conference board was appointed. Those named to serve were A. V. Miller, *New York Herald Tribune*, Samuel Kauffman, the *Washington Star*, and Irwin Maier, the *Milwaukee Journal*. These men were empowered to examine the magazine company books; one man would be replaced each year in order to give every member of the conference board an opportunity to examine operating costs.[33]

More Contract Revisions

The next contract revision occurred in 1948 and was more significant. It called for a change in the distribution of the general fund. In the future the newspapers would be reimbursed for the entire cost of the magazine, plus $1 for each thousand circulation. Any balance would then be distributed 50 percent to the newspapers and 50 percent to the Magazine Company, with the latter share limited to 10 percent of the general fund. Any year in which the $1 for each thousand circulation was not earned, the deficit would be recoverable by the newspapers in subsequent years. The conference board was given the right to change this recoverable provision if it seemed unfair to the magazine company.[34]

This Week weathered World War II, and each year after the war steadily increased in circulation and advertising volume. During the five-year period, 1945 to 1950, a gain from 6,748,353 in weekly circulation to 10,006,564 was registered with an increase in member newspapers from 21 to 28. Advertising revenue increased from $7,198,467 to $20,297,486.[35] Significant, too, was the fact that in 1950 for the first time *This Week* passed its arch-rival the *American Weekly* in both circulation and advertising. It became obvious to the publishing and advertising industries that *This Week* was a viable publishing venture.

Parade

In the meantime, another competitor began to draw the attention of the management. *Parade*, started in 1941 by Marshall Field and distributed in 12 newspapers with a weekly circulation of 1,495,676, was beginning to make progress. In 1946 John Hay Whitney purchased *Parade* for $7 million and appointed Arthur H. Motley, formerly with Crowell Collier, president. He immediately made changes in the distribution pattern, such as dropping Philadelphia, a city in which *This Week* was being distributed, and substituting cities such as Harrisburg, Pennsylvania and Hartford, Connecticut, where there was no Sunday magazine. By 1950 *Parade* had gone over 5 million in weekly circulation.[36]

Person-to-Person Editing

In 1943 Mrs. Maloney died, and Nichols was now in a position to further his theory of "person-to-person" editing of the magazine. He explained this approach as follows:

That was the background for our now generally recognized "person-to-person" editorial approach, which speaks directly to the reader—not in terms of escape but of those values which concern him most: His own ambitions and aspirations, his job, his family, his home, his community, his moral, spiritual, and intellectual values, and the society to which he belongs.[37]

Organization Changes

Soon after World War II, Covington began adding sales executives from various magazines to his New York staff. Men were attracted from all the Curtis publications, and *Redbook*, *Glamour*, *Newsweek*, and the *Herald Tribune*. Salesmen were looking to Covington for direction and bypassing Hessey who was his superior as advertising director. As a result, in 1949, when top-level changes were instituted, Hessey was moved over to vice-president and business manager, and Covington was named vice-president and advertising sales director. At the same time, Sterling was named chairman; since it was evident that relations with the newspapers were important, Cathcart was named vice-president for newspaper relations.[38]

THE EARLY 1950s

As the magazine entered the decade of the 50s, it commenced a boom period. Advertising revenue passed $20 million in 1950 and climbed steadily upward during the next five years, reaching $31,658,455 in 1955.[39] At the same time, circulation was increasing, passing the 11 million weekly average mark the same year.[40]

In May 1954, Gilleaudeau retired, and Covington was named president and chief executive officer of the Magazine Corporation. Sterling remained as chairman. From the beginning the publication had been printed in the plants of Alco-Gravure in Hoboken, New Jersey, and Chicago. In June 1954, a new plant was opened in Los Angeles to serve the newspapers on the West Coast. In later years, plants were opened in Memphis, Tennessee, and Baltimore, Maryland.

On September 30, 1955, Covington made the following announcement to all department heads and branch managers:

> The Board of Directors at its regular meeting on September 28, 1955, authorized the President to appoint Mr. William I. Nichols to the position of Publisher of *This Week Magazine* effective October 1st. In addition to his responsibilities as Editor-in-Chief, Mr. Nichols will now have an opportunity to extend his interests and activities into other departments. I am sure that he too will bring to this position many qualities which will be of great value to our company in its future operations. Mr. Sterling will, of course, continue in his capacity as Chairman of the Board.[41]

Another Contract Modification

Following the complaints of the newspaper publishers at the conference board meetings in 1947-48, another modification was added to the contract in February 1954. This addition provided that the balance in the general fund, after the newspapers received the cost of certified circulation, would be distributed as follows:

1. $1 for each thousand circulation to the newspapers (recoverable in subsequent years).
2. $1 for each thousand circulation each to the newspapers and the magazine company. This total of $2 for each thousand circulation, or part thereof, was not recoverable.
3. Balance to be divided, 75 percent to the newspapers and 25 percent to the magazine company.

The maximum share of the magazine company was to be limited to 10 percent of the general fund.[42]

Also in 1954, a new Sunday magazine, *Family Weekly*, came into being. This publication was started by Downe Publications, and it was distributed among the smaller newspapers of the country. Initially, the newspaper membership consisted of 64, with a total average weekly circulation of 1,488,428. Its first year's advertising revenue was only $298,950.[43]

Advertising Strength

As *This Week* continued to gain in advertising revenue, the most consistent and loyal advertisers were the soap companies. Procter & Gamble first tried the magazine in 1935 with a series of coupon return advertisements. In the early days, coupon returns were the fastest and most accurate method to check advertising results.[44] This first attempt by Procter & Gamble was so successful that, throughout the years from 1935 to 1950, *This Week* received every advertising promotion that Procter & Gamble sponsored. In 1935 *This Week* was twentieth in advertising revenue from Procter & Gamble, but by 1938 it had moved up to first place and stayed in first place through 1951. During this period, Procter & Gamble became the number one advertiser in *This Week*, and Colgate and Lever Brothers were close behind. By the year 1961 Procter & Gamble was spending $1,501,810 in *This Week* alone.[45]

During the World War II years, Thomas Bohan, one of the magazine's more enterprising advertising sales representatives, called on the chain drug stores and grocery stores throughout the United States gathering information on their sales and other merchandising activities. He incorporated this information into a series of studies of the trends in distribution and merchandising in the grocery and drug industries. These were presented to the trade and to advertisers every year. A point was reached where *This Week* became an authority in the grocery and drug fields and its biennial studies were looked forward to each year.[46]

The Addition of Key Market Newspapers

As the advertising volume of the publication continued to climb steadily, the newspaper relations department concentrated on soliciting key market newspapers, which were not yet in the group. The first to be signed, to begin distribution of *This Week* on October 7, 1956, was the *Denver Post* with a circulation of 362,000 and situated in one of the fastest growing markets in the country. The *Kansas City Star* stubbornly held out against signing up with a Sunday magazine for 21 years. Executives of all four Sunday supplements had made regular trips to Kansas City to attempt to make the sale. Finally, *This Week* succeeded when the *Kansas City Star*'s publisher, Roy Roberts, decided the newspaper would take the step. The starting date was St. Valentine's Day, February 1957, and the preliminary promotion advertisements in the *Star* read, "K. C. Loves T. W." in red color. This was quite a coup to add 372,000 circulation in such an important newspaper market.[47]

In addition to the *Kansas City Star*, the *Buffalo Evening News*, Omaha, Nebraska's *Sunday World Herald*, the *Grand Rapids Press*, and the *Tampa Tribune* were all added in 1957 and 1958, increasing the magazine's circulation by 1,526,982 each week. Advertising revenue passed the $30 million mark in 1955, and increased every year thereafter until it reached its highest figure, $42,810,948, in 1959.[48]

TWO NEW EXECUTIVE VICE-PRESIDENTS

Upon reaching 65 years of age in 1958, Covington began to seek a successor from outside the company. For reasons kept to himself, he did not have full confidence in those executives within. His first attempt was to hire Alden James, a former advertising sales representative at *This Week* who had left to join P. Lorillard Company (where he had spent nine years, ending up as vice-president, a member of the board of directors, and director of advertising). James rejoined the magazine as executive vice-president and advertising director in February 1957.[49]

During James' reign as executive vice-president, Covington brought in Richard Neale, who had worked at *Life* and *Sports Illustrated*. He was named assistant to the president, starting on November 3, 1958.[50] It appeared that Covington was attempting to arrange a battle for his coveted post, when on January 21, 1959, he announced to all department heads that he was bringing in Ben G. Wright as executive vice-president for administration, effective March 1, 1959. Wright was 47 years old and had been vice-president and publisher of the magazine division of Henry Holt Company.[51]

Top-level Changes

In January 1960, it was announced that Wright would head up the newspaper relations division as well as administration. That February, Covington suffered a slight stroke, and the timetable for promoting Wright to the presidency was moved ahead.[52] On May 1, 1960, Wright was elected president and chief executive officer of the United Newspapers Magazine Corporation, publishers of *This Week*. Covington was elected chairman of the board and Sterling honorary chairman. Wallace A. Sprague, who had been assistant publisher of *Parade*, was appointed executive vice-president for administration. During the same month, James resigned, and John R. O'Connor was named vice-president and advertising director and added to the board of directors. On September 20, 1960, Neale was named vice-president for sales development.[53]

An Attempt at Reader Research

Since 1950, when *Life* brought out the Alfred Politz study entitled "A Study of the Accumulative Audience of *Life*," *This Week* had been waging a difficult battle. The attempt was to combat audience figures with Audit Bureau of Circulations data, which accounted for paid circulation only, without the added bonus of pass-along readership. In the spring of 1960, Dr. Robert C. Sorensen, research director of the magazine, contracted with W. R. Simmons Company to produce, for $200,000, "A Study of Advertising Perception." *This Week* sought to establish that it had the lowest cost for each thousand readers among major weekly magazines in proven advertising communication. It was claimed that an advertisement accumulated more perceptions in *This Week* than in any other weekly magazine. Dr. Charles Raymond, technical director of the Advertising Research Foundation, stated it was one of the two most important studies that the foundation had reviewed.[54] The findings were never made public, and this may have contributed to the problems that occurred later.

Another attempt at research was suggested by the marketing department, under the direction of Raymond A. Helsel, and it was done by Market Research Corporation of America. For 20 years, this organization had provided important companies in the consumer-goods industry with information. They prepared a study for the magazine that revealed for the first time, "How much of the market for a product is accounted for by families that receive *This Week* compared to families that receive other important media?"[55] The sample consisted of 6,000 representative families selected from all parts of the United States. For a six-week period, they reported, via the diary method, on all of the print media they received and all of the television shows they viewed.[56]

This research created problems, when the sales representatives attempted to show it to advertising agencies. First, Dr. Seymour Banks, research director of Leo Burnett Co., Inc., in Chicago, objected to the study, stating that the figures were invalid. Next, Dancer Fitzgerald Sample, Inc., in New York found the results of the study "unacceptable."[57] Although the magazine's sales directors attempted to refute these charges, and continued to present the material, significance of the study was lost in the controversy.[58]

THE BEGINNING OF A DOWNWARD TREND

The new advertising rates, effective January 7, 1962, revealed the magazine at its peak. With a distribution by 43 member newspapers, the weekly circulation guaranteed in the rate card was 14,106,870.

The rate for a four-color, full-page advertisement was $56,870 and the black and white page was $49,500.[59] These were the highest print advertising page rates of any magazine to date. In the year 1962, however, a revenue loss of $3,665,449 below the previous year was incurred.[60] This presaged trouble ahead.

As advertising revenue began to decrease, management attempted several countermeasures. At the beginning of 1961, the advertising sales, promotion, and marketing departments were merged in an attempt to coordinate their important activities. At the same time they were reorganized. The sales department now had six divisions or categories with a manager over each. The categories were: automotive, drugs and toiletries, grocery, household furnishings and appliances, insurance, institutional, and tobacco. Other major magazines have since imitated this structure.[61]

Adoption of Regional Advertising Plan

Although regional advertising had been offered by all major magazines for several years, *This Week* had not yet made the move by 1961. Here again, a dichotomy existed. The management was aware of the advantages of offering a regional advertising plan to advertisers, but they also knew that the member newspapers objected to such a plan. The publishers' reasoning was that an offering of this type would divert regional national advertising from their own newspapers.[62]

Finally, figures were shown to the conference board indicating that in 1960 more than $100 million was funneled into magazine regional advertising. By 1960, 125 magazines were selling advertising on a regional basis. *Life*, for instance, had eight regions, and in the first quarter of 1961 sold $1.5 million worth of advertising in these areas. *This Week* made a presentation to the conference board on October 20, 1960 outlining a plan of five regions that would conform to the magazine's five printing plant alignments. The board responded by appointing a committee to study the problem, resulting in more delay.[63] In the meantime, advertising volume continued to decrease. By the end of 1963 it had dropped to $29,230,369.[64]

The Advertising Enigma

Early in 1962 an attempt was made to analyze the reasons behind the steady decline in advertising revenue. The principal reason was the advent of and progress made by the television industry. Television began to sell viewing time to the very same advertisers so important to the supplement. For instance, Procter & Gamble switched a large proportion of its advertising budget to television and reduced its expenditure in *This Week* to only $114,640 in 1961. From 1940 until 1959, this one account had averaged an annual advertising expenditure of $926,796 in *This Week*.[65]

Another problem for the publication was beer, wine, and liquor advertising. These accounts were unacceptable because of objections registered by a majority of the member newspapers. No advertising could be accepted without their approval.[66]

The supplement was also losing retail and direct mail advertising, again because of rules made by the member newspapers. In 1961 competing magazines sold $19 million worth of that business. It was calculated that the publication lost out on $7.9 million of drug and proprietary product advertising that was banned in *This Week* but was advertised in competing magazines. The total regional advertising expenditure in all magazines of $99 million in 1961 was also not available to the supplement.[67]

Five New Magazines

In September 1963, Covington proposed a revolutionary idea to the magazine's management and the conference board.[68] His plan was to publish five new and different *This Week* magazines. On the second Sunday of each month there was to be an expanded general edition. On the other Sundays in the month, a new, specially themed edition would be published. The titles of these would be family living, fiction, recreation, and American beauty.[69]

John J. O'Connell, former editor of *Cosmopolitan* and the *American Weekly*, was hired as executive editor to develop the new multimagazine program. He had successfully inaugurated a similar program of themed issues as editor of *Cosmopolitan* in 1956.[70]

The Death of the *American Weekly*

A weakness in the Sunday magazine field became evident in 1961. The *American Weekly* had been struggling for several years. Its advertising revenue had dropped from a high of $24,749,961 in

1957 to $7,200,701 in 1961.[71] On December 19, 1961, the *Weekly* announced that it was dropping distribution in 21 newspapers after December 31, 1961, and retaining only eight Hearst newspapers and the *Chicago American* in its group.[72]

As it became evident that *This Week, Parade,* and *Family Weekly* were too much competition, the decision was made to publish the final issue of the *Weekly* on September 1, 1963. It had lasted 67 years.[73]

Two key *This Week* executives resigned in 1963. Sprague left to accept a position as president of the Bowater Paper Company, and O'Connor went to *McCall's* as advertising director.[74] Sprague was not replaced, but Mac G. Morris moved up from assistant advertising manager to vice-president and advertising director.[75]

Newspaper Cancellations

Late in 1963, eight major newspapers submitted contract cancellations effective December 31, 1964.[76] Cancellations in the past had been kept confidential and had been rescinded before the deadline.[77] These actions sent tremors through the industry and the information reached the press.[78] *Advertising Age* and *Editor & Publisher* gave the story front page positions. Advertisers made inquiries, and several newspaper publishers in the group were concerned.[79]

The advertising salesmen were spending more time discussing the newspaper situation than selling space.[80] All of *This Week's* top executives immediately contacted each cancelling newspaper and succeeded in influencing five of them to rescind and move the notice up one year. The remaining three dropped out at the end of 1964.[81]

This defection on the part of key newspapers presented a serious problem to the management. It was difficult to trace just what triggered the mass cancellations. Some believed it was the selling of regional advertising; others thought it was caused by the multimagazine concept; and there were those who attributed it to the fact that the newspapers desired to improve or start their own Sunday magazines.[82] With the drop in circulation, advertising revenue was down from 1964 through 1968, averaging only $20 million each year.[83]

In 1964 six additional newspapers joined the earlier defectors. All but two were convinced to remain in the group. This serious situation prevailed for the next three years; finally 14 newspapers had submitted cancellations to be effective at various times.[84]

In the meantime, O'Connell was promoted to editor of *This Week* in 1965, Nichols became publisher and editorial director, and Helsel resigned to join Pepsi-Cola as a vice-president.[85]

Crowell-Collier and Macmillan Merger

On January 10, 1968, it was announced that Publication Corporation planned to merge with Crowell-Collier and Macmillan, Inc. (CC&M).[86] After the approval by the stockholders at the annual meeting on May 7, CC&M took over control of the magazine and the printing operation. Raymond Hagel, chairman of CC&M placed one of his executive vice-presidents, Joseph F. Bond, in charge of CC&M's printing and newspaper supplements division.[87]

One of Bond's first moves was to appoint Fred H. Stapleford publisher of the magazine as successor to Nichols, who was now 63, and who became senior consultant on the magazine's books program. Stapleford had been vice-president and general manager of Hugh M. Hefner Publishing Company in Chicago, publisher of *Playboy*. For 13 years he had been associated with Triangle Publications, publishers of the *Philadelphia Enquirer*.[88]

It was necessary for Bond and other top executives to make hurried trips to the member newspapers to attempt a reconciliation. As this effort was progressing, more executive changes came about. Wright resigned in March 1969 to join the Ontario Paper Company in an executive capacity. In a memorandum to department heads, he stated:

> Before you hear it from another source, I want to tell you that I am leaving *This Week* to join the Ontario Paper Company on April 1.
>
> I am turning over the direction of *This Week* to Fred Stapleford who joined us last September as publisher. When Fred has had an opportunity to review for you the plans the new management has for *This Week*, I am sure you will understand why I am optimistic about the future of the magazine.
>
> It has been a pleasure working with you over the past ten years.[89]

The New Executive Team

In August 1968, one month after Stapleford was named publisher, he brought in Alan L. Baker, of the *Philadelphia Daily News*, as vice-president for marketing to replace Neale, who had resigned to become vice-president of *Parade*. At the same time, Michael Kelly, who had been Chicago manager of the publication, was named vice-president and advertising sales director.[90] Kelly remained about two months, then left to join Newspaper I, Inc., a newspaper advertising sales organization. Kelly was replaced by Michael Jackson in January 1969.[91]

Also in January, two new editors were hired after O'Connell

resigned. They were William Woestendiek, former editor of *Newsday* and the *Houston Post* who was named editor, and Campbell Geeslin, formerly of Gannett Newspapers, Inc., who was appointed managing editor. In a promotion mailing piece, Woestendiek stated, "My job is to ring in the new, without ringing out the old. To give *This Week* renewed verve and vigor . . . while retaining . . . respect for basic values that have made it the best-loved Sunday magazine in America." [92]

At the same time, there was some encouraging news. Advertising volume was up 10.5 percent in the first quarter of 1969 as opposed to the previous year, and three new newspapers had signed contracts to distribute the magazine in Albany, New York, Stockton, California, and Huntington, West Virginia. [93]

A Desperate Effort to Save the Magazine

Although the publication advertised that it was the best-loved Sunday magazine in America, the owners were aware that all of the member newspapers did not agree. It was essential to secure assurances from the newspapers that they would continue with the magazine, at least for the next two years. That was the only manner in which advertisers could be guaranteed a delivered circulation.

The first move that CC&M made was to guarantee the newspaper publishers that their net cost would not exceed $2 for each thousand of certified circulation. This move was subsidized retroactively to January 1968. Even this did not appear to satisfy the newspapers. At the same time CC&M was investing heavily in editorial improvements and promotion. [94]

The next step taken by the magazine was more drastic. In April 1969, Stapleford sent a letter offering the magazine at no cost to all the member newspapers, provided these newspapers would guarantee distribution for at least two years. At the same time the executive staff and the sales managers made one or more presentations to 105 prospective newspapers, not already in the group. After an analysis of the results of this attempt was obtained, it was decided that, in spite of expressions of goodwill toward the effort, the necessary circulation commitment could not be attained. [95]

FINAL DAYS

In a letter to the member publishers in August 1969, Stapleford informed them that the recent offer made by CC&M had failed to attract the essential circulation base. After pointing out that 15 newspaper cancellations representing 4.3 million in circulation were already on file, and that to continue to operate the magazine would not be feasible, he wrote:

> We recommend that Sunday, November 2, 1969, be the final issue date for *This Week* magazine, and respectfully request your early agreement thereto. If you concur, please execute the enclosed release and return it to me. If you would prefer to meet for discussion, we have reserved Thursday, August 21, for this purpose.
>
> It is a pity that *This Week*, so long such a distinguished member of the newspaper family, evidently has outlasted its economic usefulness to newspapers and advertisers. Although we do not regret in any sense our determined effort to give it renaissance, we believe it would be foolhardy to continue publishing when all the vital signs are negative.
>
> Our valued associations with you and our other newspaper friends will persist. All of you who have extended such heartening advice and support have our warmest appreciation for your help.[96]

Thus ended publication of the 34-year old Sunday magazine that was the leader in the field for many years. The last issue on November 2, 1969 was 40 pages in size and contained two full-page major food companies' advertisements and two automobile advertisements. The remaining advertisements were mail-order types and less than full page in size.

The following valediction appeared on the editorial page of the magazine:

> For 35 years, the editors of *This Week Magazine* have been privileged to enter the homes of more than 20 million Americans every weekend. We have entertained, informed, amused, helped—and occasionally irritated—our readers throughout the United States. We have enjoyed being an extra member of your family.
>
> With this issue, *This Week* will cease publication, an action dictated by the economics of the publishing business.
>
> Our first—and last—goal always has been to serve our readers in the interest of a Better America. As we "strike our tent," sadly but proudly, we want you to know that we shall miss you.[97]

This left *Parade* and *Family Weekly* as the only two nationally syndicated Sunday magazines.

CONCLUSION

It is difficult to comprehend the reasons behind the demise of a magazine that ten years before had been so successful. It had led the field with over $42 million in advertising revenue and boasted the highest circulation, over 14 million, of any magazine published up to that time. Its rise and fall is essentially a marketing story. When its founders launched what was a revolutionary medium in 1935, they set a circulation goal of 4 million, through the distribution of 21 metropolitan newspapers. The magazine advanced far beyond these projections, and in 1960 its future appeared unlimited. However, a downward pressure was being felt as newspapers began to merge with competing newspapers and became the only newspaper in their respective cities. They no longer needed the competitive edge that *This Week*, as a circulation builder, offered them.

Television, which advanced rapidly in the early 1960s, began to drain off advertising revenue from all magazines, but from *This Week* in particular on account of its circulation coverage in major metropolitan areas. The advertising departments of the member newspapers were complaining to their managements that the supplement was diverting national advertising that should have been appearing in their own newspapers at full profit. The editors of the newspapers lost enthusiasm when the supplement began to average 16- and 20-page issues and became bland in content.

There was evidence of too little, too late in many instances, particularly in reference to the regional advertising sales plan and the delayed release of reliable readership studies to combat those being used by the major competitive magazines.

The parent holding company, Publication Corporation, was essentially a printing organization; every calculated production move by *This Week* was considered on its printing feasibility and not its marketing potential. *This Week* appears to have been constrained by the strict control exercised by its conference board of publishers and its member newspapers' contract regulations. Every major move had to be approved and, in the delay, the competition moved ahead.

The burdensome publishing conditions described above eventually led to the death of the magazine.

NOTES

1. Theodore Peterson, *Magazines in the Twentieth Century*, 2nd ed. (Urbana: University of Illinois Press, 1975), pp. 86-87.

2. Ibid.

3. *This Week Magazine* file, 1950-70.

4. Personal Interview with Euclid M. Covington, former chairman, *This Week Magazine*, Sharon, Connecticut, June 15, 1968.

5. Ibid.

6. Ibid.

7. Ibid.

8. John Arberry Haney, "A History of the Nationally Syndicated Sunday Magazine Supplements" (Ph.D. diss., University of Missouri, 1953), p. 169.

9. Ibid., p. 170.

10. Ibid., p. 187.

11. Covington Interview.

12. Ibid.

13. United Newspaper Magazine Corporation file, 1934-35.

14. Ibid.

15. Ibid.

16. Minutes of the Newspaper Publishers Meeting, *This Week*, Waldorf-Asortia Hotel, New York, New York, September 20, 1934.

17. Personal Interview with William I. Nichols, former editor and publisher, *This Week Magazine*, New York, New York, November 1, 1977.

18. United Newspapers Magazine Corporation file, 1935.

19. Ibid.

20. *This Week Magazine* (February 24, 1935), pp. 1-16.

21. "John Sterling Goes to *This Week* from *McCall's*," *Advertising Age* (February 3, 1936), p. 1.

22. Ibid.

23. *This Week* file, 1936.

24. *This Week* file, 1937.

25. Minutes of the Newspaper Publishers Meeting, *This Week*, Waldorf-Astoria Hotel, New York, New York, April 20, 1937.

26. *This Week* file, 1935, 1936, 1937.

27. John C. Sterling, publisher, *This Week*, address delivered to the Detroit Advertising Club, Book Cadillac Hotel, Detroit, Michigan, January 29, 1937.

28. *This Week* file, 1939.

29. Publishers Information Bureau records, 1942.

30. *This Week* file, 1947.

31. William I. Nichols, managing editor, *This Week*, address delivered to the Detroit Advertising Club, Detroit, Michigan, December 9, 1942.

32. Minutes of the Conference Board Meeting, *This Week*, Waldorf-Astoria Hotel, New York, New York, June 24, 1947.

33. Minutes of the Newspaper Publishers Meeting, *This Week*, Waldorf-Astoria Hotel, New York, New York, April 21, 1948.

34. Minutes of the Conference Board Meeting, *This Week*, Waldorf-Astoria Hotel, New York, New York, April 21, 1948.

35. Audit Bureau of Circulations Records, September periods, 1945-1950.

36. "Publishing Challenge," *Printers' Ink* (April 18, 1958), p. 30.

37. Nichols Interview.

38. *This Week* file, 1949.

39. Publishers Information Bureau records, 1955.

40. Audit Bureau of Circulations, September periods, 1950-1955.

41. Department Heads Memorandum by Euclid M. Covington, presdient, *This Week*, September 30, 1955.

42. *This Week* file, 1954.

43. Audit Bureau of Circulations Reports, September periods, 1954; and Publishers Information Bureau report, 1954.

44. John Caples, *Tested Advertising Methods*, 4th ed. (Englewood Cliffs, N.J.: Prentice-Hall, Inc., 1974), p. 10.

45. Report on Procter & Gamble Keyed Copy Advertising, *This Week*, 1935-61.

46. Personal Interview with Raymond A. Helsel, former marketing director, *This Week*, New York, New York, September 11, 1978.

47. *This Week* file, 1956-57.

48. *This Week* file, 1955-59.

49. News Release, *This Week*, February 26, 1957.

50. Department Heads Memorandum, Euclid M. Covington, president, *This Week*, October 6, 1968.

51. Ibid., January 21, 1959.

52. Covington Interview.

53. *This Week* file, 1960.

54. Memorandum to Ben G. Wright, president, *This Week*, by Dr. Robert C. Sorensen, July 15, 1960.

55. "A New Dimension in Media Selection," a study by the Market Research Corporation of America, May 8, 1962.

56. Ibid.

57. Letter to *This Week*, from Louis T. Fischer, vice-president, Dancer Fitzgerald Sample, Inc., May 21, 1962.

58. Personal Interview with John R. O'Connor, former vice-president, *This Week*, New York, New York, July 1, 1978.

59. *This Week* Rate Card, Number 35, January 7, 1962.

60. Publishers Information Bureau, 1962.

61. Sales and Sales Development Departments' Organization Chart, *This Week*, May 8, 1961.

62. Covington Interview.

63. Minutes of the Conference Board Meeting, *This Week*, Waldorf-Astoria Hotel, New York, New York, October 20, 1960.

64. Publishers Information Bureau records, 1963.

65. Ibid., 1940-61.

66. *This Week* file, 1961.

67. Ibid.

68. Covington Interview.

69. Ibid.

70. *This Week* News Release, September 26, 1963.

71. Publishers Information Bureau reports, 1957, 1961.

72. "Trimmed List for *American Weekly*," *Advertising Age* (December 25, 1961), p. 18.

73. Philip N. Schuyler, "*American Weekly* Leaves Many Ghosts," *Editor & Publisher* (July 20, 1963), p. 12.

74. Department Heads Memoranda, *This Week*, February 18, 1963; October 23, 1963.

75. Staff Memorandum, *This Week*, October 29, 1963.

76. *This Week* file, 1963.

77. Wright Interview.

78. Ibid.

79. Ibid.

80. O'Connor Interview.

81. *This Week* file, 1963, 1964.

82. Wright Interview.

83. Publishers Information Bureau records, 1964-68.

84. *This Week* file, 1964-67.

85. Staff Memoranda, *This Week*, March 10, 1965; November 5, 1965.

86. "Publication Corporation to Merge with Crowell-Collier and Macmillan, Inc.," *New York Times*, January 10, 1968, p. 41.

87. *This Week* file, 1968.

88. News Release, Crowell-Collier and Macmillan, Inc., August 19, 1968.

89. Department Heads Memorandum, *This Week*, March 18, 1969.

90. "*This Week* Loses Another Top Executive," *Editor & Publisher* (September 21, 1968), p. 21.

91. "Jackson Named at *This Week*," *Editor & Publisher* (January 18, 1969), p. 18.

92. "This isn't the *This Week* that was," Promotion Mailing Piece, *This Week*, April 10, 1969.

93. *This Week* file, 1969.

94. Press Release, *This Week*, August 13, 1969.

95. *This Week* file, 1969.

96. Letter from Fred T. Stapleford, president and publisher, *This Week*, to the chief executives of newspapers distributing *This Week*, August 13, 1969.

97. *This Week* (November 2, 1969), p. 2.

10

EPILOGUE

The purpose of this book is to trace the business management aspects of consumer magazines in the United States from 1900 to 1975. It presents in detail the economic problems faced by the magazines, which were forerunners of modern-day publications and traces the economic history of five major magazines during the twentieth century.

The early magazines in the United States were usually published by entrepreneurs who were successful in printing or newspaper publishing and who attempted to respond to the varying needs and interests of the American people. Advertising was in its infancy, and the publications were supported by subscription sales. At most, a precarious living wage was the early magazine publisher's reward.

Magazines of the eighteenth century discussed economic problems, such as do present-day publications, and they had to survive catastrophes, including wars and major political adjustments. During this era there were only seven magazines in existence in the United States. In the early 1800s weekly magazines, sectional magazines, and religious magazines were started. None of these was of lasting significance, and each changed ownership many times.

At the start of the twentieth century, there was a surge of extraordinary industrial and financial development. Of all the agencies of popular information, none experienced a more spectacular enlargement and effectiveness than magazines. These publications rode a wave of economic cyclical change. The shift from an agrarian

to an industrial economy in the United States was a stimulus for magazines of national circulation. The publishers began to take a business interest in their magazines and ceased looking upon them just as a sideline or vehicle for espousing political ideas and formulae.

National advertising, which originated in magazines, played a role in actuating modern methods of distribution of manufactured goods, and eventually became the principal source of income for magazines.

These magazines were sold at much less than cost and depended for their profit on the increase in advertising revenue. In a sense, their publishers performed a marketing function, since the advertising enabled them to play a significant, if undetermined, part in raising the material standard of living in the first half of the twentieth century.

The book concentrates on an analysis of five prominent consumer magazines. The publications chosen had some common characteristics and many that were diverse. Two of the publications proved to be highly successful, and three failed as business enterprises. Their mutuality was denoted by their popular appeal, large circulation, and high advertising page costs. One, *Better Homes and Gardens*, was a monthly publication; the others, *Life*, the *Saturday Evening Post*, *Newsweek*, and *This Week* were weekly magazines.

Magazines today face many of the same problems as those covered in this book: reader and advertiser acceptance, subscription pricing and renewal rates, advertising responses, and the development of sound financial standards.

The study of the case histories mentioned above, together with a study of the trends and forces acting upon today's magazines, in the areas listed could provide journalism students and magazine staff members with knowledge of successful efforts as background for their own future endeavors.

In order to best pinpoint the business strengths and weaknesses of the five magazines discussed, the author examined the four major areas which can offer the most useful guidance: method of operation, structural organization, decision making, and financial control.

Method of Operation.   In method of operation it was evident that all five of the publications operated under a complicated management structure. It was necessary for the publisher of each magazine to be adept at conducting a business while at the same time supervise the editorial product. Two categories of customers had to be considered at all times—the reader or subscriber and the advertiser.

The more successful publications maintained a policy of separation of "church and state" ensuring that the advertising and business departments did not interfere with the editorial program. An excellent example of this occurred when Cyrus Curtis, publisher of the *Post*, referred a powerful lobbying group to his editor, stating that he (Curtis) was merely the proprietor.

Henry Luce, realizing early in his career that magazines must have editors who have complete editorial autonomy, appointed himself editor-in-chief of all Time Inc. publications. Further, he saw to it that this autonomy was maintained for his successor, Hedley Donovan.

The appointment of the *This Week Magazine* editor had to be approved by the conference board of controlling newspaper publishers to ensure the position's independence.

Realizing that circulation growth was all important to advertising sales, the publications reported on, for the most part, made intelligent circulation gains keeping pace with realistic advertising page costs. *Life*, on the other hand, at times, increased its circulation so rapidly that it priced its advertising pages out of the market.

Structural Organization.   The structural organization of all of the magazines encompassed basic management planning processes. In all of the cases studied the magazines were part of a corporate structure. Thus, there were financial resources available to the individual magazines enabling them to pursue important plans of action.

In the cases of the three magazines that failed—the *Post*, *Life*, and *This Week*—the corporate structures were solid enough to survive. Because of their substantial financial backing and the diversification of their functions, these corporations were able to continue in business.

All of the early entrepreneurs guiding the magazines analyzed were men of outstanding courage and leadership qualities. Cyrus Curtis, E. T. Meredith, Henry Luce, Malcolm Muir, and Joseph Knapp became legends in their own time and inspirations to their staff members. They were innovators and risk takers, and led their publications through untried areas of magazine publishing.

The publisher of the magazines was the chief executive officer. Reporting to the publisher were the business manager, editor, advertising director, circulation director, marketing director, sales promotion director, production manager, and the treasurer. Each executive headed a staff carrying out functional tasks under specified standards of performance.

There were instances where boards of directors or other controlling interests hampered the decision-making role of the publisher. This occurred when the board obstructed Mathew J. Culligan in his attempt to save the *Post*. The same was true at *This Week* when the conference board of newspaper publishers exercised control over rates and the admission of new newspapers to the group, restricting innovation, progress, and growth.

Decision Making.   A requirement of effective decision making is effective decision makers. Numerous examples of key executives leading, directing, and motivating staff members were found.

The various publishers of *Better Homes and Gardens* over the years had the good judgment to reinvest profits, and at the same time diversify with investments in television, home planning institutes, and book publishing. Time Inc. made important decisions, expanding in the field of broadcasting, adding additional magazines to their corporate entity, and diversifying into the field of book publishing and paper production. Curtis executives also made justified and far-reaching decisions for many decades, resulting in the *Post* becoming America's leading magazine. In the 1960s complacency and carelessness took over. At that point, panic decisions were enacted resulting in the changing of top executives regularly and hiring others from the outside. The decision to publish libelous stories connected with two football coaches, and others, resulted in costly legal suits totaling $40 million.

Life appeared to be making all of the correct decisions, gaining in circulation and advertising revenue, until the decision in 1968 to purchase 500,000 of the *Post*'s subscriptions in an attempt to move ahead of *Look* in circulation. That move, and the attendant increase in their advertising page rate, priced *Life* out of the market and started its decline to ultimate failure.

Financial Control.   The accounting departments of the magazines studied shared a common problem: their systems had to be flexible enough to cope with the number and kinds of variables peculiar to the magazine industry. For example, the total number of their pages varied from issue to issue, as did the proportions of editorial to advertising pages. Special geographic and demographic editions also varied in circulations and pricing practices. Additionally, their production labor costs were subject to variations as a result of differing equipment availabilities and differing contractual arrangements at their printing plants. Finally, the relationship between fixed salary and overhead costs vis-à-vis constantly changing unit costs of producing and distributing the magazines also had to be considered.

In the case of the five principal magazines studied, financial control was embodied in the parent corporation. Each publisher was required to submit budgets for approval to the head of the corporation. This form of budget and operating control proved to be necessary in such large corporate magazine enterprises. Each publication had the advantage of the availability of the knowledge, experience, and expertise of the corporate heads to substantiate their own divisional decisions.

In some cases this may have hampered the individual magazine publishers in making expeditious, productive decisions. It was evident that corporate procrastination in the case of *This Week* contributed to its downfall. Research indicated that *Newsweek* maintained a sound financial structure with particular emphasis on the maintenance of a good liquid position. A centralized department for the establishment of accounting, cost, and budget controls had been established at the Washington Post Company. This organizational structure resulted in *Newsweek* becoming a solid profit center for the company.

IMPLICATIONS FOR THE BUSINESS AND MANAGEMENT EDUCATION OF JOURNALISM STUDENTS

Given the fact that there is a paucity of business and management courses offered on a regular basis at most journalism schools, this book provides clues to some interesting directions to explore. First, as a minihistory of the origins, growth, decline, and success of important magazines, it could serve as a point of departure for business journalism students to develop a clearer understanding of both the power and the perishability of the magazine product; to recognize the fact that editorial excellence alone is not sufficient for a publication's health or survival; and that well-managed, innovative business management is an essential concomitant to its success.

More specifically, journalism students could benefit from a study of the business techniques of eighteenth-and nineteenth-century magazine publishers. As Peter F. Drucker stated, "There is only one valid definition of business purpose: to create a customer."[1] A study of how customers were created in those early days, and for what purposes, could lead students to an analysis of current methods and purposes of attracting customers to magazines and to a study of trends that might affect their approach to the future.

Similarly, a comparison of magazine management diversification techniques could provide student insight into the need for a corporate structure that includes properties other than a single magazine to provide financial resources sufficient to subsidize a magazine over a difficult period, whether it be the result of editorial faltering, unanticipated business competition, or unfortunate, but correctable, marketing decisions.

The early history of the business processes of the consumer magazines around the turn of the century indicated the necessity for a thorough knowledge of management techniques. The early publishers attempted to act as editors as well as publishers of their magazines, and this resulted in failures and a meager income for many who survived. There was no national advertising and the magazines' income was confined to the subscription or direct-sale price. Early magazine entrepreneurs attempted to carry out all operations individually without delegating authority. Those managers diffused their talents by engaging in disparate projects in order to extend their fortunes.

A study of the major innovations and improved management techniques adopted by the selected magazines in the book could provide students, aspiring to careers in business journalism, with case studies of actual problem-solving approaches which, successful then, suggest exploration of courses of action germane to today's situations.

Implicit in the analysis of the five modern-day magazines researched are a number of cogent parallels in their histories and the need for thorough business management training and education. There is evidence throughout the book that magazines derived their revenue from two income streams—circulation and advertising. In the early days, without national advertising, circulation accounted for the major share of income proportion. After 1900, when national advertising began, magazines thrived on this revenue, and circulation pricing decreased to a point where publishers were selling at less than cost.

We, however, should be aware that the pendulum swung back and that modern day publishers concentrated on structuring their circulation operation to the point where its profitability was comparable to advertising. The above is another example of the need for management dexterity and awareness in business journalism training.

The personal characteristics of the leading publishers reported on in the study are worthy of exploration. As historian Allan Nevins wrote, business cannot be interpreted solely by statistics of prices and profits. These publishing executives were described in detail in many instances, and students may profit by a scrutiny of both their laudable and uncommendable characteristics.

Throughout the book the need for marketing skills in magazine publishing is apparent. The successful magazines were considered, by their publishers, as an entity, calling for skills in proper distribution, timely sales promotion, correct pricing, dynamic packaging, adequate consumer awareness through advertising, and sound salesmanship. All of these functions are worthy of consideration as bases for business management journalism courses.

Most journalism schools today still concern themselves primarily with preparing students to be editorial journalists. They are not preparing them as managers. Yet, this research sharply confirms the importance of sound business management to the success of a magazine. An investigation into the possible ways and means of requiring courses in business administration prerequisites in the curricula of journalism schools could result in the development of programs of study of more immediate and practical value to journalism students. Future journalists who understand and appreciate the principles of magazine economics, as well as those of editorial concept and execution, would be in better positions to understand and further the importance of magazines in the total communications process.

NOTES

1. Peter F. Drucker, *Management* (New York: Harper & Row, 1974), p. 61.

BIBLIOGRAPHY

Journalism Books

Allen, Frederick L. *Only Yesterday: An Informal History of the Twenties.* New York: Barton Books, 1946.

Bleyer, Willard G. *Main Currents in the History of American Journalism.* Boston: Houghton Mifflin Company, 1927.

Clark, Wesley C. *Journalism Tomorrow.* Syracuse: Syracuse University Press, 1958.

Drewry, John E. *Some Magazines and Magazine Makers.* Boston: The Stratford Company, 1924.

Ford, James L. C. *Magazines for Millions.* Cardondale: Southern Illinois University Press, 1969.

Gordon, George N. *Communications and Media.* New York: Hastings House, 1975.

Grant, Jane. *Ross, The New Yorker and Me.* New York: Reynal and Company, 1968.

Mott, Frank Luther. *American Journalism.* New York: Macmillan, 1941.

————. *A History of American Magazines.* 5 vols. Cambridge: Harvard University Press, 1958.

Peterson, Theodore. *Magazines in the Twentieth Century.* 2nd ed. Urbana: University of Illinois Press, 1975.

Regier, C. C. *The Era of the Muckrakers.* Chapel Hill: University of North Carolina Press, 1932.

Richardson, Lyon Norman. *A History of Early American Magazines, 1741-1789.* New York: Thomas Nelson & Sons, 1931.

Rubin, David M.; Sachsman, David B.; and Sandman, Peter M. *Media—An Introductory Analysis of American Mass Communications.* Englewood Cliffs, N.J.: Prentice Hall, 1972.

Tebbel, John. *The American Magazine.* New York: Hawthorn Books, Inc., 1969.

Van, Karyl; and Hahn, John. *Guidelines in Selling Magazine Advertising.* New York: Meredith Corporation, 1971.

Wolseley, Roland K. *The Changing Magazine.* New York: Hastings House, 1973.

————. *Understanding Magazines.* 2nd ed. Ames: The Iowa State University Press, 1969.

Wood, James Playsted. *Magazines in the United States*. 2nd ed. New York: The Random Press Company, 1956.

Management Books

Dale, Ernest. *Organization*. New York: American Management Association, 1967.
Drucker, Peter F. *The Effective Executive*. New York: Harper & Row, 1947.
———. *Management*. New York: Harper & Row, 1974.
Gross, Bertram M. *Organizations and their Managing*. New York: Macmillan Publishing Company, Inc., 1964.
Koontz, Harold; and O'Donnell, Cyril. *Principles of Management*. New York: McGraw-Hill Book Company, Inc., 1959.
Mason, Edward S. *The Corporation in Modern Society*. Cambridge: Harvard University Press, 1961.
Meigs, Walter B.; and Johnson, Charles E. *Financial Accounting*. New York: McGraw-Hill Book Company, Inc., 1970.
Presbrey, Frank. *The History and Development of Advertising*. Garden City, N.Y.: Doubleday, Dorn and Company, 1929.
Uris, Auren. *Mastery of Management*. Homewood, Ill.: Dow Jones-Irwin, Inc., 1968.

General Reference Books

Barzun, Jacques; and Graff, Henry F. *The Modern Researcher*. rev. ed. New York: Harcourt, Brace & World, Inc., 1970.
Best, John W. *Research in Education*. 2nd ed. Englewood Cliffs, N.J.: Prentice-Hall, Inc., 1970.
Bingham, Walter Van Dyke; and Moore, Bruce Victor. *How to Interview*. 4th rev. ed. New York: Harper & Row, 1959.
Brown, Lyndon O.; Lessler, Richard S.; and Weilbacher, William M. *Advertising Media*. New York: The Ronald Press Company, 1957.
Caples, John. *Tested Advertising Methods*. 4th ed. Englewood Cliffs, N.J.: Prentice-Hall, Inc., 1974.
Fischer, David Hackett. *Historians' Fallacies*. New York: Harper & Row, 1970.
Gorn, Janice L. *Style Guide for Writers of Term Papers, Masters' Theses, and Doctoral Dissertations*. New York: Simon and Schuster, 1973.
Gottschalk, Louis. *Understanding History: A Primer of Historical Method*. 2nd ed. New York: Alfred A. Knopf, Inc., 1969.
Kahn, Robert L.; and Cannell, Charles F. *The Dynamics of Interviewing*. New York: John Wiley & Sons, Inc., 1957.
Mattingly, Paul H. *The Classless Profession*. New York: New York University Press, 1975.
Nevins, Allan. *The Gateway to History*. Garden City, N.J.: Doubleday & Company, 1962.

Van Dalen, Deobold B. *Understanding Educational Research.* New York: McGraw-Hill Book Co., Inc., 1966.

Miscellaneous

Letters

Gould, Loyal, Chairman, Department of Journalism, Baylor University, Waco, Texas, August 31, 1976.

Speeches

McCord, Robert, Executive Editor, Little Rock, *Arkansas Democrat.* Speaking before the Association for Education in Journalism, Convention Hall, Ottawa, Canada, August 18, 1975.

Peterson, Theodore, Dean, University of Illinois, College of Communications. Testimony before the United States Postal Rate Commission, Washington, D.C., June 3, 1971.

Records

Annual Report, Publishers Information Bureau, Inc., 1950-60.

Audit Bureau of Circulations Records, September periods, 1945-77.

Magazine Advertising Bureau. *Nationwide Magazine Audience Survey: Report No. 4—Families.* New York: Magazine Advertising Bureau, 1948, 12.

Magazine Circulation and Rate Trends, 1940-74. New York: Association of National Advertisers, Magazine Committee, 1976.

Publishers Information Bureau Records, 1942-71.

Unpublished Materials

Baldwin, Deborah. "The Demise of the *Saturday Review.*" Master's thesis, University of Oregon, 1974.

Chunn, Calvin Ellsworth. "History of News Magazines." Ph.D. dissertation, University of Missouri, 1950.

Haney, John Arberry. "A History of the Nationally Syndicated Sunday Magazine Supplements." Ph.D. dissertation, University of Missouri, 1953.

Higbee, Arthur Leon. "A Survey of the Attitudes of Selected Radio and Television Broadcast Executives toward the Educational Background and Experience Desirable for Broadcast Employees." Ph.D. dissertation, Michigan State University, 1970.

Jugenheimer, Donald Wayne. "Future Communications Technology Advances and Their Principal Implications for Advertising." Ph.D. dissertation, University of Illinois, 1972.

Peterson, Theodore Bernard. "Consumer Magazines in the United States, 1900-1950, A Social and Economic History." Ph.D. dissertation, University of Illinois, 1955.

Stern, Morton P. "Palmer Hoyt and the *Denver Post*." Ph.D. dissertation, University of Denver, 1969.

Stone, Gerald Cory. "Management of Resources in Community-sized Newspapers." Ph.D. dissertation, Syracuse University, 1975.

Watson, James R. "Communication Effectiveness in University Executive Management Programs." Ph.D. dissertation, University of Illinois, 1973.

The Saturday Evening Post

Books

Bok, Edward W. *A Man from Maine*. New York: Charles Scribner's Sons, 1923.

Culligan, Mathew J. *The Curtis-Culligan Story*. New York: Crown Publishers, Inc., 1970.

Friedrich, Otto. *Decline and Fall*. New York: Harper & Row, 1970.

Goulden, Joseph. *The Curtis Caper*. New York: G. P. Putnam's Sons, 1965.

Marcosson, Isaac. *Before I Forget*. New York: Dodd, Mead and Company, 1959.

Short History of The Saturday Evening Post, A. Philadelphia: The Curtis Publishing Company, 1937.

Wood, James Playsted. *The Curtis Magazines*. New York: The Ronald Press Company, 1971.

Interviews

Caples, John, Vice-President, Batten, Barton, Durstine & Osborn, Inc., New York, New York, December 7, 1977.

Kelly, Stephen E., former publisher, *The Saturday Evening Post*, April, 1977.

Letter

Kelly, D. J., Jr., Letter in The D. J. Kelly, Jr., "Collection of Early Historical Newspapers," May 5, 1946.

Magazine Articles

Calkins, Ernest Elmo. "Fifty Years of Advertising." *Printers' Ink*, October 10, 1947, p. 26.

"Culligan's Round." *Newsweek*, December 23, 1963, p. 69.

"Curtis' Net Earnings." *Tide*, October 14, 1949, p. 30.

Maneloveg, Herbert D. "*Post* Gives Lesson in How Not to Market a Magazine." *Advertising Age*, February 10, 1969, p. 56.

"New Bundle of Hope for Ailing *Post*." *Business Week*, May 25, 1968, p. 42.

"*Post's* Death Haunts Him." *Advertising Age*, January 26, 1970, p. 1.

"Special 'Post' for Execs Tells Circulation Plan." *Advertising Age*, June 10, 1968, p. 1.

"View From the 9th Floor." *Newsweek*, April 2, 1962, p. 62.

Newspaper Articles

Bedingfield, Robert E. "Feb. 8 Issue of *Saturday Evening Post* to be Last." *New York Times*, January 11, 1969, p. 1.

"Two Directors Quit at Curtis and *Post.*" *New York Times*, February 13, 1969, p. 1.

"Curtis Sales Staffs United." *Wall Street Journal*, August 23, 1968, p. 1.

Dougherty, Philip H. "Curtis Turns Over an Old Leaf." *New York Times*, July 8, 1973, p. 15.

Fosburgh, Lacey. "*Saturday Evening Post* to Reappear as a Quarterly." *New York Times*, November 6, 1970, p. 47.

Lee, John M. "Curtis Publishing Has a New Format." *New York Times*, April 1, 1962, p. 1.

MacDougal, A. Kent. "*Saturday Evening Post* After a Long and Stormy Search for a New Image." *Wall Street Journal*, November 16, 1964, p. 4.

"Magazine Publisher Sees Brighter Days." *Detroit News*, April 4, 1963, p. 1.

New York Mirror, November 15, 1828, VI, p. 151.

Saada, Michael J. "Magazine Rate Increase." *Wall Street Journal*, October 11, 1947, p. 1.

"Time Inc. to Lend Curtis Publishing Co. $5 Million and Give It Other Assistance." *Wall Street Journal*, May 20, 1968, p. 1.

Welles, Chris. "*Post*-Mortem." *New York*, February 10, 1969, pp. 32-33.

Miscellaneous

Curtis Publishing Company files, 1949, 1960, 1962.

Curtis Publishing Company News Release, August 31, 1964.

Harvard Business School. *The Saturday Evening Post*. Case History, Number 6-373-009, 1972, 17.

Better Homes and Gardens

Interviews

Burnett, Robert A., President, Meredith Corporation, New York, New York, August 24, 1978.

Curley, Hugh, Research Director, *Better Homes and Gardens*, New York, New York, December 1, 1977.

Rehm, Jack D., Publisher, *Better Homes and Gardens*, New York, New York, December 9, 1977.

Schaefer, Otto G., former New York Advertising Director, *Better Homes and Gardens*, Scarsdale, New York, July 3, 1978.

Letters

Jones, W. F., former New York Advertising Director, *Better Homes and Gardens*, January 30, 1978.

Zosel, Kenneth P., Administrative Manager, *Better Homes and Gardens*, Des Moines, Iowa, August 3, 1978.

Magazine Articles

"Bailey Leaves Meredith for LHJ Ad Post." *Advertising Age*, February 3, 1972, p. 1.

Better Homes and Gardens I, July 1922, p. 3.

"*Better Homes and Gardens* Forms Reader Panel for Product Tests." *Advertising Age*, January 19, 1976, p. 1.

"*Better Homes* Stresses Its Image." *New York Times*, February 6, 1973, p. 90.

"*Better Homes* to Reduce Size of Page in '77." *Advertising Age*, January 5, 1977, p. 1.

Dougherty, Philip H. "Advertising Enthusiast." *New York Times*, July 6, 1970, p. 49.

Ebert, Larry Kai. "Meredith at 75." *Advertising Age*, October 31, 1977, p. 78.

Fowler, Elizabeth M. "Inflation Worries Most Consumers But They Lack a Plan to Combat it." *New York Times*, April 8, 1968, p. 73.

"Meredith and Drake University Team-up for Magazine Seminar." *Imprint*, Spring, 1977, pp. 6, 7. A publication of the Meredith Corporation.

"Meredith Borrows $23 Million to Convert *Better Home's* Format." *Wall Street Journal*, December 31, 1975, p. 1.

"Meredith Starts a New Magazine." *Des Moines Register*, April 13, 1922, p. 1.

"Your Home Is Where Our Heart Is." *Better Homes and Gardens*, September, 1947, p. 27.

Records

Better Homes and Gardens fiftieth anniversary file, October, 1972.

Better Homes and Gardens files, 1928, 1956, 1972.

Better Homes and Gardens News Bureau file, August 1, 1947.

Meredith Company records, October, 1971.

Newspaper Article

The New York Times, October 11, 1964, p. 1.

Unpublished Material

Reuss, Carol. "*Better Homes and Gardens* and its Editors: An Historical Study from the Magazine's Founding to 1970." Ph.D. dissertation, The University of Iowa, 1971.

Speeches

Burnett, Robert, President, Meredith Corporation, address delivered to *Better Homes and Gardens* Advertising Sales Conference, Innisbrook Hotel, Innisbrook, Florida, November 10, 1977.

Miller, Wayne, Vice-President and General Manager, Meredith Magazine Division, address delivered to *Better Homes and Gardens* "Five-Oh" Sales Conference, Maui, Hawaii, January 25, 1972.

Newsweek

Interviews

Beebe, Frederick, former Chairman, Newsweek, Inc., New York, New York, July 21, 1972.

Bradlee, Benjamin, former Washington Bureau Chief, *Newsweek*, Washington, D.C., December 15, 1972.

Callaway, L. L., Jr., former Publisher, *Newsweek*, New York, New York, July 10, 1972.

Davis, F. E., Senior Vice-President, Newsweek, Inc., New York, New York, January 21, 1977.

Harriman, Averell, New York, New York, February 5, 1967.

McCabe, Gibson, former President, Newsweek, Inc., New York, New York, January 11, 1977.

Muir, Malcolm, former Publisher, *Newsweek*, New York, New York, October 27, 1976.

Thompson, Harry, former Publisher, *Newsweek*, New York, New York, August 3, 1972.

Letter

Robinson, J. Bay, Partner, Whitman Ransom & Coulson, New York, New York, December 17, 1964.

Magazine Articles

"A Blank Check for Roosevelt." *News-Week*, February 17, 1933, p. 5.

Moley, Raymond. "After 25 Years and Six Days." *Newsweek*, November 3, 1958, p. 112.

Newspaper Articles

"Frederick Beebe Dies at 59; Chairman of *Washington Post*." *New York Times*, May 2, 1973, p. 48.

"Philip Graham Dies; *Newsweek* Publisher." *Herald Tribune*, August 4, 1963, p. 1.

"Philip L. Graham Dies; Victim of Long Illness Takes Own Life at 48." *Washington Post*, August 4, 1963, p. 1.

Salisbury, Harrison E. "*Washington Post* Buys *Newsweek*." *New York Times*, March 10, 1961, p. 1.

"Two Magazine Mergers Are Announced." *Wall Street Journal*, February 10, 1937, p. 5.

Memoranda and Reports

Martyn, T. J. C., Memorandum to the Editor of *Newsweek*, New York, New York, October 23, 1934.

Newsweek Executive Officer Memorandum to the staff by Malcolm Muir, July 13, 1956.

Newsweek files, 1933, 1941, 1953, 1958, 1961, 1963, 1966.

Newsweek Masthead, February 12, 1945, p. 2.

1978 Fact Book, The Washington Post Company, p. 12.

The Washington Post Company 1975 Annual Report, The Washington Post Company, Inc., p. 9.

Weekly Publications, Inc., *Newsweek Contract*, with Newspaper Guild of New York, January 16, 1939.

N/w. (House Organ of Newsweek)

N/w., Newsweek, Inc., October 8, 1961, p. 1.

N/w., Newsweek, Inc., March 1, 1969, p. 1.

N/w., Newsweek, Inc., March 25, 1971, p. 1.

N/w., Newsweek, Inc., March 24, 1972, p. 1.

N/w., Newsweek, Inc., May 4, 1973, p. 1.

N/w., Newsweek, Inc., May 30, 1975, p. 1.

N/w., Newsweek, Inc., May 7, 1976, p. 1.

Life

Books

Elson, Robert T. *Time Inc.* New York: Atheneum, 1968.

Hamblin, Dora Jane. *That Was the Life.* New York: W. W. Norton & Company, Inc., 1977.

Interviews

Hardy, Jerome S., former Publisher of *Life*, New York, New York, October 25, 1978.

Heiskell, Andrew, Chairman, Time Inc., New York, New York, November 21, 1978.

Jackson, C. D., Publisher of *Life* and Bruce, Lee, *Newsweek* Reporter, New York, New York, April 11, 1961. Copy in *Newsweek* file.

Letter

Eggleston, George T., Editor, *Life*, New York, New York, October 7, 1936.

Magazine Articles

"A Prospectus for a New Magazine." *Tide*, September, 1936, pp. 3-8.
"Continuity Study." *Tide*, November 1, 1940, p. 13.
"How Big is *Life*?" *Tide*, April 28, 1950, p. 76.
"*Life* Cuts Back." *Newsweek*, October 12, 1970, p. 130.
"*Life*, The Year in Pictures 1972." *Life*, December 29, 1972, cover.
"*Life*." *Time*, October 19, 1936, p. 62.
"*Life* Regrets Demise of *Look*, but Eyes Ad Dollars." *Advertising Age*, September 27, 1971, p. 1.
"*Look* to Fold." *Advertising Age*, September 20, 1971.
"The Current Fad for Picture Magazines." *The Literary Digest*, January 30, 1937, p. 19.
"The Good Old Ways." *Newsweek*, December 13, 1971, p. 74.
"The Lingering Death of *Life*." *Newsweek*, December 18, 1972, pp. 109-10.
"Valk Becomes *Life* Publisher." *Advertising Age*, December 15, 1969, p. 1.

Newspaper Articles

Dallow, Robert E.; and Lawrence, John F. "Real-*Life* (& *Look*) Melodrama." *Washington Post*, December 29, 1970, pp. C1-C2.
Dougherty, Philip H. "Advertising: *Life* Mobilizes Sales Battalion." *New York Times*, September 21, 1967, p. 77.
"Advertising: *Life* Salesmen Get Pep Talk." *New York Times*, April 30, 1970, p. 70.
"Henry Luce, 68, Dies in Phoenix." *New York Times*, March 1, 1967, p. 1.
Hill, Gladwin. "Howard Hughes Tells of His Life in a 3,000-Mile Phone Interview." *New York Times*, January 10, 1972, p. 1.
"*Life* Magazine Is Eliminating 80 to 90 Jobs." *New York Times*, December 2, 1971, p. 43.
"*Life* Plans Circulation Cut." *Washington Post*, November 25, 1971, p. 17.
MacDougall, Kent. "Time Inc.'s *Life* Magazine Says it Will Cut Circulation 1.5 Million." *Wall Street Journal*, October 2, 1970, p. 49.
Robinson, Douglas. "Hughes Files Suit Here to Block Publication of 'Autobiography.'" *New York Times*, January 14, 1972, p. 30.
"What's Ahead for *Life* and *Look*?" *Media Decisions*, February, 1971, pp. 40, 43, 44.
Whitney, Craig R. "Rhodes Files Suit Against *Life*, Seeking $6.3 Million for Libel." *New York Times*, April 17, 1970.

Speech

Luce, Henry R., President, Time, Inc., address delivered to the American Association of Advertising Agencies, The Greenbrier Hotel, White Sulphur Springs, West Virginia, April 15, 1937.

Records and Files

Life files, 1937, 1938, 1939, 1941, 1942, 1943, 1944, 1945, 1946, 1947, 1948, 1949, 1956, 1960, 1961, 1962, 1963, 1964, 1971.

Life, Magazine Publisher's Statement, Audit Bureau of Circulations, for six months ending December 31, 1969.

News Release, Life Magazine, Inc., October 7, 1936.

Time Inc., *Annual Report*, 1937, p. 4.

This Week Magazine

Interviews

Covington, Euclid M., former Chairman, *This Week*, Sharon, Connecticut, June 15, 1968.

Helsel, Raymond A., former Marketing Director, *This Week*, New York, New York, September 11, 1978.

Nichols, William I., former Editor and Publisher, *This Week*, New York, New York, November 1, 1977.

O'Connor, John R., former Vice-President, *This Week*, New York, New York, July 1, 1978.

Letters

Fischer, Louis T., Vice-President, Dancer Fitzgerald Sample, Inc., May 21, 1962.

Stapleford, Fred T., President and Publisher, *This Week*, to the chief executives of newspapers distributing *This Week*, August 31, 1969.

Magazine Articles

"Jackson Named at *This Week*." *Editor & Publisher*, January 18, 1969, p. 18.

"John Sterling Goes to *This Week* from *McCall's*." *Advertising Age*, February 3, 1936, p. 1.

"Publishing Challenge." *Printers' Ink*, April 18, 1958, p. 30.

Schuyler, Philip N. "*American Weekly* Leaves Many Ghosts." *Editor & Publisher*, July 20, 1963, p. 12.

"*This Week* Loses Another Top Executive." *Editor & Publisher*, September 21, 1968, p. 21.

This Week Magazine, February 24, 1935, pp. 1-16.

This Week, November 2, 1969, p. 2.

"Trimmed List for *American Weekly*." *Advertising Age*, December 25, 1961, p. 18.

Newspaper Article

"Publication Corporation to Merge with Crowell Collier and Macmillan, Inc." *New York Times*, January 10, 1968, p. 41.

Speeches

Nichols, William I., Managing Editor, *This Week*, address delivered to the Detroit Advertising Club, Detroit Athletic Club, December 9, 1942.

Sterling, John C., Publisher, *This Week*, address delivered to the Detroit Advertising Club, Book Cadillac Hotel, Detroit, Michigan, January 29, 1937.

Memoranda and Files

Covington, Euclid M., President, Memorand to Department Heads, *This Week*, September 30, 1955; October 6, 1958; January 21, 1959.

Department Heads Memoranda, *This Week*, February 18, 1963; October 23, 1963.

Department Heads Memorandum, *This Week*, March 18, 1969.

Sorensen, Dr. Robert C., Memorandum to Ben G. Wright, President, *This Week*, July 15, 1960.

Staff Memoranda, *This Week*, October 29, 1963; March 10, 1965; November 5, 1965.

This Week files, 1935-1970.

United Newspaper Magazine Corporation files, 1934-35.

Miscellaneous

"A New Dimension in Media Selection," a study by the Market Research Corporation of America, May 8, 1962.

List of Charter Member Newspapers.

News Release, Crowell Collier and Macmillan, Inc., August 19, 1968.

News Release, *This Week*, February 26, 1957.

News Release, *This Week*, September 26, 1963.

News Release, *This Week*, August 13, 1969.

Report on Procter & Gamble Keyed Copy Advertising, *This Week*, 1935-1961.

Sales and Sales Development Departments' Organization Chart, *This Week*, May 8, 1961.

"This Isn't the *This Week* That Was," promotion mailing piece, *This Week*, April 10, 1969.

This Week Rate Card, Number 35, January 7, 1962.

Minutes of Conference Board Meetings and Publishers Meetings

Minutes of the Conference Board Meeting, *This Week*, Waldorf-Astoria Hotel, New York, New York, June 24, 1947.

Minutes of the Conference Board Meeting, *This Week*, Waldorf-Astoria Hotel, New York, New York, April 21, 1948.

Minutes of the Conference Board Meeting, *This Week*, Waldorf-Astoria Hotel, New York, New York, October 20, 1960.

Minutes of the Newspaper Publishers Meeting, *This Week*, Waldorf-Astoria Hotel, New York, New York, September 20, 1934.

Minutes of the Newspaper Publishers Meeting, *This Week*, Waldorf-Astoria Hotel, New York, New York, April 20, 1937.

Minutes of the Newspaper Publishers Meeting, *This Week*, Waldorf-Astoria Hotel, New York, New York, April 21, 1948.

APPENDIXES

APPENDIX A:

Tentative Interview Outline

Following is an example of a tentative interview outline with topics identified through a preliminary search of the literature, and arranged in chronological order, with an attempt to phrase them to elicit the freest possible response:

1. What was the early business management purpose of your magazine?
2. What were the early business strategies, objectives, priorities, and work assignments of your publication?
3. Who were the early business management executives of your organization, and what was the design and content of their executive positions?
4. What social problems were encountered as the magazine progressed, and how were these resolved into business opportunities?
5. During the history of your magazine, how did management changes evolve, and what were the results of these changes?
6. Peter Drucker defines a manager as one in a position of responsibility for the work of others. How did your managers in the past carry out this responsibility?
7. Have there been any mergers or acquisitions by your firm over the years, according to your recollection, and have these proven successful ventures?
8. What innovative and modern business management techniques have been instituted in your magazine organization in recent years?

APPENDIX B:

Letter by D. J. Kelly, Jr., in the D. J. Kelly, Jr., "Collection of Early Historical Newspapers"

America's First Newspaper

The D. J. KELLY, Jr. *Collection of Early Historical Newspapers*

DANIEL J. KELLY, Jr.
619 NORTH ST. LOUIS BOULEVARD
SOUTH BEND 17, INDIANA

May 5th.

Newsweek,
Broadway and 42nd St.,
New York 18, N.Y.

Gentlemen:

The Saturday Evening Post is America's oldest magazine, but it was not founded 218 years ago. Some years ago the Post dropped from its cover the unfounded claim that it was established in 1729 by Benjamin Franklin.

The Post was started as the "Bee" by Howard S. Coffin in 1821. After several months of publication it passed to Charles Alexander, who with Samuel C. Atkinson, issued the newspaper under the name of the Saturday Evening Post. Vol.I, No.1 was published August 4, 1821, and in 1897 it was purchased by Cyrus H. K. Curtis, who built it up as a national magazine.

Benjamin Franklin purchased the Pennsylvania Gazette in 1729. It had been established the year before by Samuel Keimer, but had not been successful. The Gazette became popular under Franklin's ownership, and in 1766 his partner, David Hall, took over as sole owner. Later he was joined in the firm by William Sellers.

The Gazette was discontinued with the issue of October 11, 1815 after the deaths of Hall and Sellers. The type and equipment were scattered among the various printing offices of the city of Philadelphia long before the Saturday Evening Post was established. This makes it difficult to trace the Post back to either Franklin or the year 1729.

Sincerely yours,

D. J. KELLY, JR.

A PANORAMA OF THE AMERICAN PRESS FROM ITS BEGINNING . . . AND HIGHLIGHTS OF THE GREAT HISTORICAL EVENTS OF OUR NATION

APPENDIX C:

Letter from J. Frank Seaman, Promotion Manager, the *Saturday Evening Post*, to Newspaper Editors, May 22, 1942

★ THE SATURDAY EVENING

POST *Independence Square, Philadelphia*

May 22, 1942

Gentlemen:

Enclosed is a copy of The Saturday Evening Post of May 30.

This is a precedent-smashing issue, as you will discover, and therefore we felt you would like to have a copy in advance and for your own use.

Changes which Ben Hibbs, editor of the Post has had in the making for some time begin to be apparent with the May 30 issue. Just to highlight these changes for you there is the new logotype, which sets the pace for the changes inside in make up and content. There is new type dress inside and particularly noticeable is the fact that articles are shorter and more numerous. This particular issue carries five short stories, seven articles, two serials in addition to editorials and features. The art layouts of both fiction and articles have been enlivened. There will be further improvements along similar lines as the weeks pass.

Your attention is called particularly to the article "This War Will Save Private Enterprise" by Thurman Arnold on page 24. This provocative article possibly has news value and if you think so permission is granted to quote up to 500 words from it, in papers of Wednesday, May 27, or thereafter.

Sincerely,

J. Frank Seaman

The Curtis Publishing Company

THE SATURDAY EVENING POST · LADIES' HOME JOURNAL · COUNTRY GENTLEMAN · JACK AND JIL

APPENDIX D:

Letter from Curtis Publishing Company Executives to M. Albert Linton, Chairman of the Executive Committee, September 29, 1946

PERSONAL AND CONFIDENTIAL

September 29, 1946

Mr. M. Albert Linton, Chairman
The Executive Committee
The Curtis Publishing Company
4601 Market Street
Philadelphia, Pennsylvania 19139

Dear Mr. Linton:

The undersigned, as you may know, constitute the effective operating management of the Curtis magazines. All of us have devoted years to our profession and years to the Curtis Publishing Company, which we now see in jeopardy as the direct result of mismanagement and questionable behavior on the part of Mr. Culligan.

We are, quite frankly, in a state of revolt on the simple moral premise that we cannot, in good conscience, continue to contribute our skills and our reputations to what we view as an immoral deception of our fellow employees, our readers, our loyal advertisers, the directors and the stockholders of Curtis.

We fear that the Board of Directors has been deluded by Mr. Culligan and is unaware of the many instances of questionable and perhaps even illegal conduct of the company management. There have been shocking instances of advertising kickbacks, which we understand may be illegal under the Robinson-Patman Act. There have been consistent misrepresentations to us and to the public of the truth about the company's extremely bleak financial position. There has been consistent frivolous waste of the company's funds by Mr. Culligan and a coterie of men around him—and this in the face of a certainly disastrous profit and loss statement. Most recently, Mr. Culligan offered to "buy off" two dedicated company officers, Mr. Blair and Mr. Kantor, with a settlement involving sums in the hundreds of thousands of dollars in exchange for their agreement to leave the company quietly. We believe this is unethical.

We know of numerous incidents of similarly questionable conduct and plain mismanagement. We feel it is our duty to inform you, as Chairman of the Executive Committee of the Board of Directors, of these incidents and of our moral revulsion. We are confident that the board, once informed, will act to impose a responsible and ethical management on the company.

In our view, outward evidence of a management explosion in Curtis at this point could very well be fatal to the company. Therefore, we suggest that Mr. Culligan be quietly stripped of his executive power, but left nominally in charge for the sake of appearance only, at least until an internal investigation of the legality of some of his more questionable actions has been completed. In his place we suggest an executive committee be formed headed by yourself and including Mr. Blair, Mr. Kantor and Mr. Poppei. We feel that this committee, if appointed by the Board, should act immediately to implement a plan to save the corporation, a plan which exists and to which Mr. Culligan has paid only lip service. In our judgement, these magazines and the company can be saved if all of us, working with the plan and under an ethical management, continue to devote to them the energy and dedication we have demonstrated in the past.

On the other hand we are convinced that the company and the magazines face ruin in the very near future if such steps are not taken immediately.

Individually we are determined to bring this to your attention in a last effort to correct the situation. If nothing is done to correct it, none of us, as a matter of individual conscience, feels that he can continue to participate in what he knows to be deceitful and wrong. In each case, we are determined to terminate our employment with the company if the status quo is maintained.

We do this with full awareness that our action will undoubtedly cause sufficient loss of reader and advertiser confidence to kill the Curtis publications and thus kill the company. Obviously, we hope that this will be unnecessary. But we prefer to see these great institutions die with honor than expire, as they are now doing, under a corrupt leadership.

Marvin D. Kantor
Chairman
Magazine Division

Clay Blair, Jr.
Editor-in-Chief, Editor
The Saturday Evening Post

William A. Emerson
Managing Editor
The Saturday Evening Post

Otto Friedrich
Assistant Managing Editor
The Saturday Evening Post

Norman R. Ritter
Assistant Managing Editor
The Saturday Evening Post

Hank Walker
Assistant Managing Editor
The Saturday Evening Post

Charles Davis Thomas
Editor
Ladies' Home Journal

Caskie Stinnett
Executive Editor
Ladies' Home Journal

Don A. Schanche
Editor
Holiday

Jesse L. Ballew, Jr.
Publisher
The Saturday Evening Post

John Connors
General Sales Manager
The Saturday Evening Post

Barth Hite
Advertising Director
Holiday

J. Michael Hadley
Publisher
Ladies' Home Journal

John L. Collins
Publisher
American Home

APPENDIX E:

Letter from Martin S. Ackerman, President, The Saturday Evening Post Company, to the Employees, January 10, 1969

THE
SATURDAY
EVENING
POST 58 PARK AVENUE
NEW YORK CITY, N.Y. 10016
COMPANY PHONE 212-686-2728

MARTIN S. ACKERMAN PRESIDENT

January 10, 1969

Dear Fellow Employee:

By this time you will have learned that The Saturday Evening Post will cease publication with the February 8, 1969 issue.

Today is undoubtedly one of the saddest of my life. Having taken the responsibility for pulling The Post out, I must take the responsibility for closing the magazine. Because of the individual efforts of so many of you, it seems to me that you are entitled to know the reasons for this reluctant decision.

You have heard me say that we needed 1,000 advertising pages for The Post in 1969 to realize a profit for The Post of approximately $1,000,000. Well, it appears evident that we will be down at least 10% from that minimum target; perhaps more if current adverse conditions throughout the magazine advertising business continue. All books for 1969 look to me as if they will be off 1968 levels, which were not good. That 10% therefore would have meant a loss of more than $3,000,000 for 1969.

Having refinanced The Saturday Evening Post Company with $15,000,000 in new capital, I assured Directors and Stockholders of the Company that regardless of my personal feelings, if we could not return a profit we would have to shut down The Post.

Why couldn't we realize a profit? The answer is not simple, but it seems to me that we just could not sell enough advertising and cut expenses fast enough. I must say that the advertisers, especially the agencies, have been with us 100%, but our needs were just too great for what was available to us from the total dollars to be spent. Editorially, we have done a good job of living up to our earlier promises. Apparently there is just not the need for our product in today's scheme of living.

 / **HOLIDAY** / Status

We hope to make the shut-down as easy as possible -- but it's hard, no matter what I say. Details will be forthcoming.

Would I do it again? My answer is, "Yes." We are constantly forced to make decisions which severely affect our lives, but it is not the choice alone which is important; it is our effort in trying to do what may have seemed impossible that is important.

My personal thanks for your individual help which made this decision involving the life of America's great Saturday Evening Post even more difficult.

Sincerely,

Martin S. Ackerman

APPENDIX F:

Newsweek Contract

AGREEMENT made this thirteenth day of January 1939, by and between Weekly Publication, Inc., a New York corporation, hereinafter referred to as the Publisher, and the NEWSPAPER GUILD OF NEW YORK, a local of the American Newspaper Guild, hereinafter referred to as the GUILD, acting for and on behalf of itself and of all regular editorial department employees except bona fide executives, hereinafter called Employees of the Newsweek magazine, which is published by the Publisher.

1. HOURS. There shall be a five-day week of forty hours.

2. OVERTIME. The Publisher shall grant employees equal time off for overtime for the first four (4) hours of overtime worked in any one week in excess of forty (40) working hours. For all overtime in excess of forty-four (44) working hours, overtime shall be compensated for at the rate of time and half in cash. When compensated for in time the liquidation of overtime shall be made at intervals of not more than three (3) months.

Hours worked shall be recorded on forms or by such methods as may be adopted by the Publisher in order to conform with the Wages and Hours Law.

3. MINIMUM WAGES. The following schedule of minimum wages shall prevail during the term of this agreement, effective as of January 1, 1939. Experience as used herein shall mean experience on Newsweek or Time magazine or the previously published Literary Digest.

(Listing of position names and
minimum wages followed)

4. SEVERANCE PAY. Any dismissed employee employed for six (6) months or more shall be paid a lump sum of money, determined on the basis of his average salary for the preceding six (6) months of service prior to the discharge, which lump sum of money shall amount to two (2) weeks' pay computed as herein specified for employees who have been employed for less than one (1) year but more than six (6) months.

5. VACATIONS. Publisher agrees to grant annual vacations with pay as follows: Two (2) weeks' vacation annually after six (6) months or more of employment during such year. Writers who have

been employed six (6) months or more shall receive three (3) weeks' vacation annually.

6. SICK LEAVE. The policy of the Publisher with regard to sick leave and disability shall continue as at present.

7. SUPPLIES AND EQUIPMENT. The Publisher shall follow his present practice in the provision of working supplies and equipment.

8. NO PAY CUTS. The Publisher agrees that there shall be no reduction in pay of any employee and no discharges or layoffs during the life of this contract as a result of putting this contract into effect.

9. GRIEVANCE COMMITTEE. A shop adjustment committee composed of not more than five (5) Guild members, at least one of whom shall be an employee of Newsweek magazine and all of whom shall be selected by the Guild, shall be established for the purpose of presenting to the Publisher or its representative any grievance arising under this contract with a view to its amicable adjustment.

10. DURATION. This agreement shall remain in full force and effect for a period of one (1) year from date.

Not earlier than sixty (60) days prior to the expiration of this agreement either party hereto may give to the other party written notice of a desire to change the terms thereof, and in the event of such notice, negotiations respecting such desired changes shall be immediately entered into and shall proceed with all due diligence. If an agreement has not been reached by the date upon which this agreement expires, status quo conditions shall be maintained during negotiations.

IN WITNESS WHEREOF, the parties hereto or their duly authorized agents have duly executed the foregoing agreement.

Dated the 16th day of January, 1939.

WEEKLY PUBLICATIONS INC.

s/Malcolm Muir
_____
President

NEWSPAPER GUILD OF NEW YORK

WITNESSED BY:

s/Milton Kaufman
_____
Executive Secretary

John E. Pfeiffer
Gerson Zelman
Robert G. Whalen

s/Ed C. Schneider
_____

APPENDIX G:

Graham's Check to the Vincent Astor Foundation

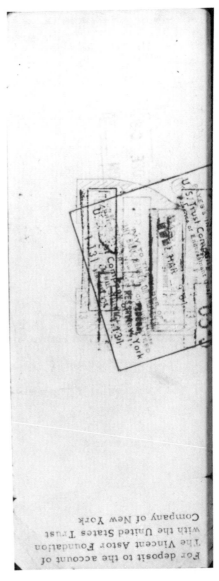

APPENDIX H:

Letter from George T. Eggleston, Editor, *Life*, to S. T. Williamson, Editor, *Newsweek*, October 7, 1936

Life

LINCOLN BUILDING
60 EAST 42ND STREET
NEW YORK, N.Y.

October 7th, 1936.

Mr. S. T. Williamson, Editor
News-Week
Rockefeller Center
1270 Sixth Avenue
New York City

Dear Mr. Williamson:

Inclosed is an announcement by Clair Maxwell, publisher of Life, marking the termination of the fifty-three year career of the magazine as a humorous publication.

Your use of this material will be appreciated.

Sincerely yours

George T. Eggleston

EDITOR

George T. Eggleston
aj
Inc.

APPENDIX I:

This Week Magazine Charter Newspaper Members

The *Atlanta Journal*
The *Baltimore Sunday Sun*
The *Birmingham News*
The *Boston Herald*
The *Buffalo Times*
The *Chicago Daily News*
The *Cincinnati Enquirer*
Cleveland Plain Dealer
The *Dallas Morning News*
The *Detroit News*
The *Sunday Star*
  (Washington)

The *Indianapolis Sunday Star*
The *Commercial Appeal*
  (Memphis)
The *Milwaukee Journal*
The *Minneapolis Journal*
The *Item-Tribune*
  (New Orleans)
Herald Tribune (New York)
Omaha World-Herald
Philadelphia Record
The *Pittsburgh Press*
St. Louis Globe-Democrat

INDEX

ABOUT THE AUTHOR

WILLIAM PARKMAN RANKIN is financial and insurance advertising manager of *Newsweek* magazine. Prior to this position he was general manager of the Newsweek Feature Service. Before joining *Newsweek* he held executive positions at Time Inc., *This Week Magazine*, *Redbook Magazine*, and the Gannett Corporation.

Dr. Rankin has written *Selling Retail Advertising* and *The Technique of Selling Magazine Advertising*. Dr. Rankin holds a B.S. degree from the School of Journalism at Syracuse University, and an M.B.A. and Ph.D. from New York University. He is a member of Delta Pi Epsilon Business Education Honorary Fraternity, Sigma Delta Chi, and Alpha Delta Sigma. He is also a member of the New York Dutch Treat Club and Winged Foot Golf Club. He is married to the former Ruth E. Gerard and lives in Larchmont, New York, and Bomoseen, Vermont.